changing rooms

changing rooms

LINDA BARKER

Photography by Shona Wood

BBC BOOKS

This book is published to accompany the television series *Changing Rooms*,
which is produced by Bazal Productions Ltd for BBC TV.

Executive producer: Linda Clifford
Producers: Pauline Doidge and Ann Hill

Published by BBC Books,
BBC Worldwide Ltd, Woodlands,
80 Wood Lane, London W12 0TT

First published 1997
Reprinted 1997, 1998 (twice)
© Linda Barker and Bazal Productions Ltd 1997
The moral right of the author has been asserted.

Rooms designed by: Linda Barker, Laurence Llewelyn-Bowen,
Anna Ryder Richardson, Liz Wagstaff and Graham Wynne
DIY Handyman: Andy Kane

ISBN 0 563 38382 8

Designed by Jane Forster
Edited by Jane Donovan
Styling & Art direction of photography by Jane Forster
Photographs by Shona Wood © BBC Worldwide Ltd 1997
Illustrations by Terry Evans © BBC Worldwide Ltd 1997

Printed and bound in Great Britain by Butler & Tanner Ltd, Frome and London
Colour separations by Radstock Repro Ltd, Midsomer Norton
Jacket printed by Lawrence Allen Ltd, Weston-super-Mare

Cover illustrations:
Front (top): Mexican Kitchen
Front (bottom): Feng Shui Bedroom
Back: Turquoise Bedroom

contents

INTRODUCTION 6
THE DESIGN TEAM 7
DESIGN BASICS 8

introduction

Changing Rooms is, in theory, a very tempting proposition for anyone who hankers after an exciting new look for a tired old environment. Someone else pays for the decorating and you get a whole new room in just a couple of days. And, best of all, your friends or neighbours have to do all the hard work. Sounds great, doesn't it? Be warned . . .

The budget is strictly limited to £500 and I can assure you that there have been some pretty hair-raising last minute 'design modifications' made to ensure that we keep within that £500. While two days might seem to pass rather leisurely if all you have to do is to paint a couple of walls and iron the curtains, it goes by at an alarming speed when you have to clear, clean, re-design, re-decorate and re-furnish an entire room without scumble glazing the camera crew by mistake. You have to leave your beloved home in the dubious hands of two design-crazed neighbours, egged on to fever pitch by an interior designer, who will never have to even visit again once they've finished the room, let alone live with it! However, there is one consolation. For almost every waking hour of the two days that each programme takes to film, you'll be kept so busy working on your neighbours' room that there will be hardly an idle moment to worry about little things like where you will cook if you hate your new kitchen, where you are going to hide if your friends hate their new bedroom and, of course, how you can get new neighbours without having to move house.

If there's one thing which our programme puts to the test, it's just how well you actually know your oldest friend or closest neighbour. What would you really do to their favourite room if you could get your hands on it and what would they do to yours? That's the beauty of *Changing Rooms*. It's not just about paint, fabric and techniques, it's to do with people, friendship and ideas – grand ideas, great schemes and bold plans that work brilliantly (with some luck).

As an interior designer, *Changing Rooms* has given me a unique opportunity to witness at first hand just how different individual decorating tastes have now become and how universally popular good design still is. Every room is a new challenge, with its own shape, light, function and potential. Into this space we bring the tentative ambitions of our two amateur decorators and the informed enthu-siasm of an unsuspecting professional. From here on, the race begins. Handy Andy and the programme's team of designers are there to show each couple how to achieve all the effects that they have always wanted to try out and then to help them complete it all in two short days. As you can tell from the programmes, it's often a hard slog to keep on schedule – especially when it all starts to go wrong – but there are invariably some hilarious moments to keep us all laughing and there's nothing like an impossible deadline to get things done.

It would be dishonest to say that everyone fell instantly in love with their new room but I know for sure that we've left more than a few tearful celebra-tions in progress. Whether this was from pure plea-sure or grateful relief, I was never completely certain. As for the rooms themselves, they have each been as different as the teams who created them. Every one of the designers has their own personal favourites (and nightmares) and this book has finally given me the chance to pick some highlights from the first two series for you to take in at your leisure. I can only hope that you get as much pleasure out of revisiting them as we got from creating them and, with a bit of luck, they might just inspire you to do some *Changing Rooms* of your own.

Linda Barker

THE DESIGN TEAM

Meet the designers who work their magic on the interiors featured in *Changing Rooms*:

LINDA BARKER

Originally a fine artist, Linda quickly established herself as an interior designer. Her work ranges from private commissions in the homes of celebrities to writing for magazines, and she has also written almost a dozen books. Her most recent title is *Just Junk*. As well as working on *Changing Rooms*, Linda is a resident designer on BBC1's *Change That*.

ANDY KANE

'Handy' Andy has worked as a carpenter and joiner ever since he left school and got his City and Guilds qualifications. He has worked on a wide range projects, including work for Richmond Theatre. Andy came to public notice (and earned his nickname) as the man who kept BBC2's *Changing Rooms* going and since then he has worked on a range of other television programmes including *Change That*.

LAURENCE LLEWELYN-BOWEN

Laurence originally trained as a fine artist in London, but since then he has turned to the world of interiors. He began by painting murals but his repertoire now ranges from sumptuous theatres, aircraft and millionaire mews houses in Mayfair to sitting rooms, bedrooms and kitchens designed on a £500 budget for television's *Changing Rooms*.

ANNA RYDER RICHARDSON

After working as a professional model and then as a fitness instructor, Anna now specializes in designing children's rooms. She has also appeared on a number of television programmes, most recently BBC1's *The Terrace* and *Change That*.

LIZ WAGSTAFF

Liz first trained as a graphic designer and then moved on to theatre design. Her first job was as a set designer for a touring opera company. She then spent four years as curator of Knebworth House where she studied restoration and went on to design interiors for private clients. Liz has appeared as an interior designer on BBC's *Changing Rooms*, *Change That* and *Good Morning with Ann and Nick*. She lives in London and is currently in the process of writing her third book.

GRAHAM WYNNE

Graham started his career as a theatre designer and is now one of London's top interior designers and stylists. He has worked on a range of projects for some of the biggest names in the fashion business, designing interiors to match each season's look, but some of his biggest challenges have come as a designer on *Changing Rooms* and *Change That*.

design basics

It is important for any designer to be aware of colour, pattern and texture, and how these work together in a space. The combination can make a brilliant design. Design is an unpredictable equation that is not always easy to pinpoint as designers have their own criteria, ways of selecting colour and highlighting details. *Changing Rooms* hopefully gives you an insight into our way of thinking a scheme through from the minute a colour goes on the wall to placing the last accessory.

COLOUR CONFIDENCE

Here, bright blue emulsion paint was applied directly onto the prepared woodwork. Combined with green and yellow accessories, it is a good example of harmonious colours working well together.

This is undeniably the most important element of a room scheme but invariably, it is almost always the biggest problem that people have. When it comes to choosing a colour for a room, many people simply cannot decide what to do and often reach for the nearest tin of

pastel or shade of white. Admittedly, even for a designer, colour is not always an easy choice. Look at the colours around you. Consider not only the furnishings or carpet, but also the accessories in the room ranging from fruit in a bowl to colours in pictures.

Start with the colours that you like the most. Choosing a colour is so often what you love instinctively, whether it is the colour of faded denim or a rich purple damask. Find elements that contain these colours and study them carefully. Look at books and magazines too. Follow your instincts and remember that there's no one else to please except yourself (and perhaps other people in your house). Trust your choice and remember that what one person calls garish may be another's favourite colour.

Bearing all this in mind, however, there may be special circumstances in which a colour couldn't work. Pure yellow in a north-facing room with little daylight can often appear muddy and drab (see page 49). Often the bright, purer colours from far-flung climates may not work in the same way as they did when saturated in strong sunlight. Study a room at various times of the day to assess just how a colour can behave under different circumstances. Paint boards with sample colours and take these into the room at different times of the day and look at them under various lighting conditions to help you to make the right choice for your own home.

THE COLOUR WHEEL

There are a few devices used for looking at colour and colour combinations. A traditional colour wheel is an arrangement of colours separated into six basic shades seen in a rainbow. On the wheel, the colours are brought around to meet in a circle. The six colours are blue, red and yellow (primaries) and violet, orange and green (secondaries). Colours that lie between them are tertiaries – for example, turquoise lies between blue and green while crimson is a mixture of violet and red. Primaries, secondaries and tertiaries can be built up into a twelve-colour wheel, each colour

gradually blending into its neighbour.

The wheel has a useful role to play in designing and creating successful interiors. A flash of a complementary colour can really lift a colour scheme and prevents one colour from becoming too dominant. Look at the magenta pink chair covers and curtain swags set against the powerful green in our room in Penistone (see page 40). The colours are opposite on the colour wheel and naturally discordant but they can create a vibrant effect and, when handled correctly, this can work brilliantly. Harmonizing colours are next to one another on the colour wheel. In an interior your eye can pass easily between these colours to make a softer scheme. Think of the parchment wall colours combined with rich golds and ochres in our music room (see page 16). Using harmonies or complementaries can be a very useful way of looking at and selecting colour and when you understand colour, then you can use it to help your design.

Colours that lie opposite each other on the colour wheel (right) are complementary to one another. The shock of magenta pink (above) in this green bedroom illustrates how effective a splash of a complementary colour can be in the overall scheme.

CREATING YOUR OWN DESIGN BOARD

Once you have established the colours you like, start to put the elements together. Test out small areas of colour using watercolours or crayons first. Use whatever is to hand. Add a little white to tubes of colour to make a shade lighter or deepen the tone with a touch of a complementary colour. Now get the paint chart out and hold this against the colours you have blended together. Match a paint tone with an area of colour that you particularly like and the choice of paint colour suddenly becomes more bearable and that much easier.

Although it often becomes a huge hurdle to get over, paint is just one aspect of interior decoration. Other considerations include fabrics, lighting and floor treatments. If you are planning to change the soft furnishings, ask for small fabric samples or use scraps of old fabrics, if you have them. Take bigger samples for those areas that require lots of fabric such as curtains and smaller samples for accent colours that you may be thinking of using, for accessories such as cushions or a small rug.

It may be that your design board inspires larger projects in the room. We used natural twigs as a decorative display in this green glass vase (left) but I was also inspired to use bundles of twigs around the stems of floor lights. The chandelier (right) helped to bring the whole design scheme together in the attic room in Penistone.

Paint samples and scraps of fabric are the most obvious items to use when putting together a design board but don't be afraid to use colours from a piece of china or a collection of photographs. These too evoke a certain mood or feeling that may be useful when planning your overall design scheme.

PUTTING SAMPLES TOGETHER

Use these samples in a practical way to give yourself a real idea of how they are going to work in a room. If the curtains are intended to be full with swathes of fabric, try bunching up your sample to give an impression of how this will look. Place it against a paint sample and start to build up a sample board. Do the two work together? Is the contrast too great? Do you need to tone down the wall colour to get a more harmonious scheme? Once you start to put all these elements together, you can begin to build up a picture of how things will look.

I often find that natural materials may inspire an element of the design. Place pieces of granite, china or stone on the board next to the paint and fabric to see how these colours and textures work together. I used twigs, pebbles and pieces of bark to determine the colour scheme in our Belsize Park living room (see page 34). The design scheme benefited not only from the natural colours of these elements but they were also used in a physical way too. Hanging a branch from the ceiling proved to be an innovative lighting treatment and while this may not be to everyone's taste, beautifully shaped pebbles or a piece of sculptural driftwood, for example, can have a place in almost any room.

Remember: this is the time to experiment. The next stage is buying the paints and fabrics for real and mistakes can cost money. If you have only ever dreamed of putting lime green and orange together, then do it here on a sample board where it costs nothing to dabble.

LIGHTING

In any room, lighting can affect the feel and space enormously. If you do nothing else, simply fix a dimmer switch onto your existing lighting system to see how this can affect a room. There are several types of lighting that need to be considered in any home:

GENERAL LIGHTING

This is often the central pendant fitting and it is usually rather dull, but with a little inspiration it can become more inspiring. Think of the unique chandelier in Penistone (see page 46 and above).

TASK LIGHTING

In this case the lighting needs to be well-positioned and directed – a study lamp on a desk, for example.

ACCENT LIGHTING

This kind of lighting often uses spotlights to highlight an area or a display.

INFORMATION LIGHTING

For safety and control, you need information lighting, such as on the porch or stair light, where it is placed to prevent accidents. Remember that light affects colour so always view paint and fabric samples in the room itself under the lighting conditions that will be used.

ORGANIZING YOUR SPACE

The information that follows is largely written from a personal perspective but there are theories about where things should go and certainly, in kitchens and for work spaces there are rules of ergonomics that are designed to help our lives become more tolerable and efficient. For example, just how much space is required around a dining chair or what is the critical distance between sink, fridge and cooker in a busy kitchen? This can make the difference between space working well or not at all.

FENG SHUI

Designers have recently become aware of the powerful principles of Feng Shui. This is an ancient Chinese wisdom that goes back at least 4,000 years and it has become a fashionable new design trend. In Asia it is a vital part of everyday life.

Well-situated furniture is thought to be extremely auspicious. An example of questionable Feng Shui in the kitchen is to position the cooking area too near to the dishwashing space (fire and water clash). In the Feng Shui Bedroom (see pages 64–71), the balance of yin and yang, and light and dark helps promote auspicious Feng Shui.

COLLECTIONS

For those with their own collections, whether prints, flowers or ornaments, focal points can be provided in a room either by displaying collections on walls or arranging them on table tops. Trivial objects often gain importance by being displayed together (see Liz's Nautical Attic Room on pages 104–111, where boat-yard paraphernalia makes such a

strong visual impact). These items can often really start to pull a scheme together. On a kitchen dresser, jars of preserves or pasta can be used as a practical display. Glass bottles and containers can also work well in a bathroom.

Above: Our dark green room in the Isle of Dogs is an example of the Feng Shui philosophy. Here, light against dark and matt surfaces against shiny ones can be seen.

Left: Rather than putting a picture above the fireplace, I hung three small stringed instruments that I found elsewhere in the room.

CREATING NEW LOOKS FROM OLD MATERIALS

Good economic advice for those on a tight budget is to make the most of what you already have. In the Arts & Crafts Room (see page 51), the old carpet was lifted to reveal a near-perfect original Victorian tiled floor. Junk furniture too can offer surprising results. The painted armoire (right) started life as two shabby drawer and cupboard units.

When you need to change everything, it's likely that your well-earned money has already been spent by the time it comes to furniture. However, your old dresser can be given a complete transformation with a lick of paint and a bit of polish – look at the pine dresser in the Mexican Kitchen (below right). Paint old picture frames or, better still, gild them for a new look that doesn't cost the earth.

Salvage yards are a bonus for anyone who is thinking of redecorating. Although usually confined to London, one can find them in other parts of the country – I've often visited an excellent one in Yorkshire. Salvage yards contain all manner of furniture and eccentricities. The best bargains often turn up at car boot sales and you can always haggle over the price. Don't forget to take a look in charity shops too. Much to the chagrin of 'Handy Andy', I've sometimes presented him with more than a challenge to make something out of some piece of old tat. Check nearby skips (particularly if a house is undergoing a conversion) but make sure you ask the owners first. Contrary to the widely held belief, good can nearly always come from bad – just check for woodworm first!

Above and right: Create new pieces of furniture from pieces of junk which can be picked up inexpensively or transform a piece of furniture that you already have in your home. You'll be amazed at what a lick of paint can do!

room styles

Above: An exciting mix of colours, patterns and textures gives this living room a light, airy look. It has been designed for someone with a slightly unconventional style. Personal mementos and original artworks add character to the room.

Right: This is an impressive and elegant treatment for a master bedroom. A solid wall colour is lifted with a delicate, filigree stencil at ceiling height while gold-embroidered sari fabrics give an unexpected Asian influence.

Below: A sophisticated bedroom using a controlled palette of colours. Crisp whites are used to balance the strong pink and turquoise colours. The result is an elegant sanctuary away from the turmoil of day-to-day living – somewhere to rest, relax and unwind.

Above: Hot spicy colours were used to evoke this Mexican-inspired kitchen. Brightly coloured ceramics further enhance the style, along with dried chillies, limes and strings of dried herbs.

Left: A vibrant, decorative treatment is used for this multi-purpose space. All the accessories cleverly evoke the nautical theme: from the clock which is set into a lifesaving ring to the calico rug with painted signal flags.

attic MUSIC ROOM

Once a nursery, the top floor rooms of Fulbeck Hall are now a cosy residence for musicians Sally and Mick. On the understanding that they were looking for a small flat, they were given the details of Fulbeck Hall. They approached the 'small flat' through a wrought-iron gate and drove along a tree-lined driveway to find the impressive Fulbeck Hall at the end of it. When they discovered that the flat was one small part of the magnificent building, they immediately fell in love with the place.

Michael and Mary, owners of Fulbeck Hall who worked with me on the room, had strong ideas about the decoration. 'Light, parchment colours,' advised Mary, 'with a painted ceiling to reflect the open sky.' Michael had been an accomplished graphic designer before the house became his full-time work and he was looking forward to painting musical references on the walls or ceiling. He too wanted to evoke a kind of celestial atmosphere for the room. They both felt that the flat had the feeling of being up in the clouds and this should be the dominating theme.

I was more than happy with their design ideas and looked forward to working on a large-scale mural. A sourcebook gave me the image that I was looking for – a splendid golden sun with rays extending outwards in all directions. By transferring the image onto the wall with the projector, we could trace off the outline directly onto the wall, then fill in the gilded details later on.

Left: An MDF sun with three small halogen recessed bulbs replaced the original hanging pendant light (right). Together with airy parchment colours, it brought together the celestial feeling in the finished room.

GETTING STARTED

Parchment colours were to be used as a foil for the more dramatic sun face and as a perfect background for Sally's rather beautiful pictures, paintings and mosaics.

DESIGNER'S INSPIRATION BOARD

The celestial images worked well with the lilac-painted ceiling which was given a soft, cloudy sky effect (we used Blue Day). The halogen lights were fitted to a dimmer switch so that at night they could be switched down low to look like starlight.

Michael and Mary had requested parchment colours and as soon as the emulsion was applied, the room appeared to be much more spacious and full of light. The glazes that were applied afterwards had the effect of warming the base colour (an important consideration bearing in mind how cold these rooms were during the winter). The sun-shaped mural, with its glittering metallic paint, radiated at least the illusion of more heat. Michael's design skills were put to good use to paint in the details of the sun. Mary applied the gold paint and was delighted not to be painting a mural on the ceiling. Her sympathies were with Michelangelo, but then he did have four years to paint the ceiling of the Sistine Chapel.

COLOUR WASHING THE WALLS & WOODWORK

The walls and panelling had been rag-rolled and as the colour was a little dominant, we decided to paint over this using a colour wash:

■ Sand the walls and woodwork lightly with a medium-grade sandpaper on a power sander, then apply a base (we used one-coat

The soft parchment colours provided a perfect background colour for the strong graphic quality of the sun motif.

CHECKLIST

DAY ONE:

- Protect floor carpet with dust sheeting
- Base coat walls and panelling
- Apply first and second coats of glaze
- Paint ceiling
- Project sun face onto wall and paint
- Sew curtain panels and paint panels
- Cut timber for table and bench
- Dye throws in washing machine

DAY TWO:

- Finish painting mural
- Gild glazing panels for shutters
- Hang curtain poles
- Paint, gild and limewax bench
- Limewax table
- Dry sofa throws
- Paint the violin 'bridge' onto an adjacent wall

PAINTING THE CEILING

As the colour of the ceiling was previously white, I chose to let parts of this ghost through the lilac colour (Blue Day) for a cloudy effect:

■ Use undiluted colour with a 7.5cm (3in) brush in a scrubbing technique. Once the ceiling is dry (about an hour), clouds can be emphasized using the same technique with white emulsion.

Magnolia emulsion). Use a roller to apply the paint, cutting in with a 5cm (2in) brush.

■ Colour wash the walls (we used two matchpots of Tawny Desert and Ming Gold). Tip the emulsion into a paint kettle and pour in the same amount of acrylic scumble glaze. The glaze extends the drying time of the emulsion so that it can be worked longer and the opaque paint colour becomes semi-translucent. This is perfect for building up layers of different colours as they start to ghost through one another.

■ Mix the paint thoroughly with the glaze using an old paintbrush, then apply the glaze with a 7.5cm (3in) brush. Dip the brush ends into the glaze and scrub into the surface of the walls. Work outwards in all directions until the glaze starts to dry (about two to three minutes) and a cloudy effect develops. Work over the walls and woodwork in the same manner.

■ Apply the second glaze in the same way, building this colour over the first. Aim to build up a depth of colour to make a textured paint surface.

Sally and Mick had an impressive collection of musical instruments and these were displayed together in a corner of the room.

SUN MURAL & GILDED MIRRORS

The combination of the sun mural, clever lighting on the ceiling and the gilded mirrors really brought the celestial style to life.

Although the sun mural looks complicated, it is quite simple to recreate:

Copy an image of a sun from a copyright-free source onto a sheet of transparent film (use a photocopying bureau for this). Place on an overhead projector, secure with masking tape and switch the machine on. Move the projector until the sun image is accurately placed on your wall.

Mix up a little emulsion colour on a saucer with an equal amount of water and use a stiff, fine artist's bristle brush to carefully trace around the dark lines cast by the projector. Build up the face of the sun gradually using a myriad of tiny dots and speckles and use longer brush strokes for other parts of the design. Leave the emulsion paint to dry for about an hour.

A stiff-bristled artist's brush is used to draw in the graphic lines of the sun. The facial features are built up from tiny dots of paint applied rapidly with the point of the brush. Dots applied closer together create darker shaded areas.

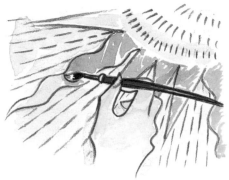

■ Finally, mix together an equal amount of gold powder with clear cellulose varnish to create a rich, highly metallic gold paint. Use this to fill in the sun's rays with a larger artist's brush. The paint will dry in about 15 minutes. Clean the brushes with cellulose thinner.

GILDED SHUTTER MIRRORS

Glass panels were cut to size by a glazier and then decorated:

■ Splatter the glass with a mixture of white polish and spirit wood dye (we used Dark Oak) and a 7.5cm (3in) brush. This will dry in about 20 minutes. Spray the glass surface with spray adhesive and apply decoupage images (from a copyright-free sourcebook) right side

MATERIALS & EQUIPMENT

MURAL	
Sun image	Saucer, for mixing
Transparent film	Fine artist's bristle brush
Overhead projector	Gold metallic powder
Masking tape	Cellulose varnish
Emulsion colour (Andean Grey)	Large artist's brush
	Cellulose thinner

down onto the glass. Spray with adhesive again, then press Dutch metal leaf over the decoupaged surface to cover the whole of the glass.

■ Dry-brush the excess away. Leave for two hours. Protect with spray polyurethane varnish. Leave to dry for an hour and secure the gilded side of the shutter mirrors to the shutters with panel adhesive.

The shutters are designed to be closed up at night so that the gilded surface softly reflects the light from inside the music room.

In place of curtains, calico wall hangings (60cm/24in) wide were hung at the windows to drop just inside the window seat. They were decorated with fabric paints and a permanent black marker pen, then hung from curtain poles for a decorative effect.

You could copy the images shown here or source your own from copyright-free reference books.

PUTTING THE LOOK TOGETHER

Finally, Andy made a rustic table, and some wonderful drawings, paintings and musical instruments were mounted on the walls to complete the decorative effects.

RUSTIC BENCH & TABLE

The timber used by Andy was purchased in a salvage yard:

■ To make the bench, saw four upright posts ranging from 1.2m (4') to 1.5m (5') high. Shape the ends with finials using a jigsaw and a power drill fitted with an extra large bit. Mark the bench height on the four posts. Then, with the two back posts on the ground, mark the back rest on these pieces in pencil.

■ Cut four lengths of 5 x 5cm (2 x 2in) timber for the seating framework. (Two lengths equal to the depth and two lengths equal to the width.) Use long screws to secure the timber onto four upright posts, with the exception of the back section. To do this, drill and countersink holes and secure with screws.

■ Cut fretwork slats for the vertical backrests using 10 x 2.5cm (4 x 1in) boards. Draw shapes on equal lengths of board. Cut out with a jigsaw. Secure the slats into the bottom edge of the backrest and top edge of the seat framework. Drill and countersink holes. Join the pieces together with long wood

screws. Screw this section onto the main framework. Cut shaped arm rests and fix these in position in the same way.

■ Rest 10 x 2.5cm (4 x 1in) timber boards across the seat. Cut these around the uprights at each corner with a jigsaw. Screw onto the framework to secure in place. Sand with coarse-grade paper fitted onto the power sander.

There is something very tactile and appealing about battered old timber. You will find that it costs much less than if it were new and perfectly finished. Make sure you sand any rough bits smooth before painting or waxing.

Paint parts of the bench with coloured emulsion (we used Lime Green). Leave to dry for one hour and gild (see page 21). Apply lime wax (see page 59).

■ Construct the table-top sides from 10 x 2.5cm (4 x 1in) timber cut to size. Screw the sides down onto a 6mm (¼in) MDF top (turn the table upside down). Predrill and countersink holes/rawlplugs.

■ Secure four legs (cut from 7.5 x 7.5cm/3 x 3in timber), one at each corner. Each leg is set back from the corner. Use pre-drilled, countersunk holes. Turn the table over.

■ Measure the table top from the outside timber edges. Have a piece of toughened safety glass cut to this size. Panel-pin lengths of wooden moulding (mitred with a block) along the table sides allowing the top edge of this to be flush with the glass top.

■ Sand the table with coarse sandpaper. Limewax, then buff. Fill the display area and drop the glass in place.

FINISHING TOUCHES

Additional softness was added to the room by the sofa throws which were dyed green and used to recover the sofa.

Pictures and mosaics were rehung and some musical instruments were displayed as clever artworks on the walls. Whilst the room was styled, Michael painted the bridge of a violin onto the wall to reflect Sally and Mick's musical interests. Sally and Mick were stunned by the total transformation of their room and felt compelled to simply sit down and take it all in.

The deep recessed area of the table enabled large items, such as a candlestick and a plant pot, to be displayed.

master
BEDROOM

Mary and Michael's home is a rather modest one – in terms of stately homes, that is. Fulbeck Hall stands on acres of beautiful gardens and peacocks strutted obligingly across well-manicured lawns when the *Changing Rooms* team arrived. For Laurence Llewelyn-Bowen, it was a dream come true: together with neighbours Sally and Mick, he was about to undertake the decoration of a master bedroom in Mary and Michael's private quarters. As they belonged to the English Heritage Trust, Mary and Michael devoted much of their time to keeping the parts of the house that were open to the public well maintained and immaculate. Consequently, they never seemed to have the time to decorate their own part of the house. However, they were more than happy to give Laurence a free rein.

Once the majority of the antique pieces had been moved out of the room and he could start painting, Laurence enjoyed himself enormously. The colour scheme that he agreed on with Sally and Mick was bright yellow walls with black gloss woodwork and black stencilling. A powerful base colour was needed to display the dark walnut, mahogany and fruitwood furniture, together with collections of china. Vibrant yellow achieved this brilliantly: it showed off the antiques but it also had the effect of flooding the room with a warm, sunshine colour.

Opposite: Saffron yellow saris allowed the light to filter through, whilst heavier black drapes framed the windows. The room was brought back to an elegant style which was far removed from its humbler beginnings (right).

GETTING STARTED

Sally and Mick, who worked on the room with Laurence, knew how cold the room could be. They wanted to use a colour that could warm you up just by looking at it.

DESIGNER'S INSPIRATION BOARD

Bright yellow interiors were fashionable during the nineteenth century when yellow pigment first became available. It was often combined with black, and sometimes a warm red, in many neoclassical interiors.

Laurence was familiar with the work of Sir John Soane. Soane was an English architect who became a leading influence in the classical revival in England. As a result of this, Laurence chose to use a play of light against dark patterns on the stencilled yellow walls.

One of the most famous of all yellow rooms is Monet's home in Giverny, France. Here the dining room is painted in a vivid, powerful yellow and has provided inspiration for many designers and decorators. As at Giverny, where prints were displayed against the yellow walls, Laurence used the vibrant yellow to show off paintings, needlework and china collections.

PAINTING THE WALLS & ROUNDEL

Two coats of emulsion (we used Cornfield) were applied to the walls with 10cm (4in) brushes. Some of the original moiré wallpaper still showed through, as Laurence intended. The ceiling was left white.

Laurence plotted out the large roundel which filled almost the whole ceiling:

■ Secure a piece of string to the centre of the ceiling with a small nail which is, in turn, tied onto the end of a long stick with a pencil tied to the end of the stick at the required radius for your roundel. Keeping the string tight and the pencil in contact with the ceiling, hold the stick and walk round in a circle to mark out the shape.

The design board illustrates how two powerful colours (in this case, black and rich yellow) can work brilliantly together to create a striking impression.

CHECKLIST

DAY ONE:
- Clear room
- Paint walls
- Plan out and paint roundel on ceiling
- Paint woodwork
- Polish floorboards with black polish
- Cut and paint fretwork overdoors
- Cut stencils for curtain and cornice
- Begin stencilling

DAY TWO:
- Gild door panels
- Finish stencilling
- Make up dress and sari curtains
- Stencil fabric
- Sew bobble edging on sari curtains
- Make up pelmet boards
- Make up mosaic
- Recover fabric screen

CREATING THE FRETWORK DOORS

Laurence designed fretwork pieces to be used over the bedroom doors:

■ Draw out overdoor shapes onto graph paper using French curves (available from graphic design stores). Transfer to 6mm (¼in) MDF by placing carbon paper on top of the MDF, put graph paper on top and trace over in pencil.

■ Follow the carbon outlines to cut out with a jigsaw fitted with a narrow blade (see pages 148–9). Smooth with medium-grade sandpaper. Apply a coat of dark grey undercoat. Leave to dry for two hours then paint with black gloss.

■ Secure the overdoors in place with panel adhesive. Emphasize the panel details of the doors with solvent-based metallic paint (we used Gold).

■ Fill in the roundel with a coat of primer and whilst this is still wet, brush in the sky effect. Use 7.5cm (3in) brushes to paint in two overlapping colours (we used Atlantic Blue and Magnolia in eggshell). Paint first in one direction and then the other, to build up an uneven layer. Leave overnight to dry.

Laurence used the graphic qualities of black against rich yellow for maximum visual impact. The doors were keyed and then primed with grey primer and one coat of black gloss was applied. Black furnishing wax (Liberon) was applied, using shoe brushes, to the floorboards, which were then buffed up with soft cloths.

EXOTIC CURTAIN TREATMENT

A formal curtain treatment was used to create an impression of sheer luxury in this beautifully proportioned room.

Floor-length black drapes contrasted with lightweight yellow saris to create a stately mood. To make your own:

■ Remove the curtains from their tracks and hand-stitch dress lining material over the top of the heading. Prior to this

White cotton pompom edging is dyed black and then stitched along the leading edge of the undercurtain sheers.

first stencil the leading edge with gold fabric paint (see page 55). Fix the sides of the lining to the original curtains with Wunda Web. Allow the hem to hang loose, simply use Wunda Web to turn back the lining hem to the inside. Rehang the curtains.

■ Make sheer fabric drapes to hang behind the heavier drapes from yellow sari fabric. Measure and cut according to the height of your window, one width of sari fabric equals one curtain width. Allow an additional 5cm (2in) for seams at top and bottom. Turn the allowance over at the top and bottom and sew with running stitch on the machine. Repeat for the other curtain half. Dye cotton pompom fringing in black machine dye (follow the instructions on the package). Once dry, straight stitch pompoms to the leading edge of each sari curtain by hand or machine.

■ To dress the window tops, Andy fixed pelmet boards made from MDF: the length being the width of the curtain heading and the depth is the distance from the wall to the front of the curtains plus 2.5cm (1in) for clearance. Each board is 25cm (10in) high. Drill the walls with a

MATERIALS & EQUIPMENT

Dress lining material (one width for each drape)
Sewing needle and thread
Gold fabric paint and stencilling brush
Scalpel, manilla card and cutting mat (for the stencil)
Black-and-white source material
Iron-on fabric bonding (Wunda Web)
Yellow and black embroidered saris
Retractable tape measure
Tailor's chalk
Dressmaking scissors
Pompom fringing

Black machine dye
Fabric glue
Velcro
Jigsaw (for cutting pelmet board)
6mm (¼in) MDF (length equals curtain width plus 2 returns and width is 100cm/4in)
Power drill with masonry bit
Power screwdriver, rawlplugs and small screws
Fixing blocks
Staple gun
Decorative metal tiebacks

power drill and insert rawlplugs into the holes. Screw the MDF pieces together and use fixing blocks to secure to the wall. Attach self-adhesive Velcro along the pelmet boards. Stitch Velcro to the sari tops. Secure to the top of the pelmet keeping the top edge straight and covering the returns of the pelmet board. The curtains and the saris were held back with decorative metal tiebacks. Cut the decorative end off the black sari. Arrange the black sari in a swagged drape on the pelmet board and staple into place. Then take the reserved sari end and scrunch up into an attractive shape. Staple to the pelmet centre.

On this pelmet, the gold-embroidered sari edge was used to good effect but plain colours also produce excellent results for a rich and luxurious look. Pelmets are a perfect way to lift otherwise quite plain and uninteresting curtains. Decorate according to the style of your room. Swags can be caught back with bows, rosettes or more sculptural tails. For simpler shapes, use a single swag and catch this unobtrusively at the side of the curtain.

Sari fabrics are generally sold as fixed lengths. Traditionally, the richly decorated part of the sari is displayed at the front of the garment.

PUTTING THE LOOK TOGETHER

All the antique furniture was returned to the room, with few changes in the original arrangement but with such a dramatic change overall.

MOSAIC FIRE SCREEN

Sally had been working on a mosaic panel as a gift for Mary and Michael and she felt inspired to finish this off for the room. To make your own mosaic:

■ Measure the aperture for the mosaic and jigsaw a piece of 6mm (¼in) MDF to this size. Seal both sides with a solution of one part water to PVA adhesive. Apply with a 7.5cm (3in) brush and leave until the adhesive dries clear (about an hour). Draw on the outlines for the mosaic. Scratch the board using the sharp teeth of a tenon saw to roughen the surface for the mosaic.

■ Cut tile or ceramic pieces using tile nippers. Hold between finger and thumb and place the cutting edge of the nippers over the edge. Squeeze the nippers together. Fix the pieces onto board with waterproof wood adhesive.
■ Use waterproof grout to fill in the spaces between the tiles. Spread and work this over the surface with a rubber blade spreader until each gap is filled. Wipe away the excess grout. Leave to dry overnight, then buff with a clean, dry cloth. Fix into a frame or screen.

ORIENTAL PANELLED SCREEN

Laurence covered two screen panels behind the bed with dark midnight blue dress lining fabric:

■ Measure the height of the screen, add 5cm (2in) and cut the lining. Use the lining width to fill one screen width. Fold the seam allowances under at top and bottom and press in place. Pin the fabric carefully to the top of one screen panel,

Above: Sally worked on her own design for the mosaic for several days before our arrival.

Below: This delicate stencil was applied around the room at cornice level. Spray paint speeds the job along enormously.

The rich, dark coloured antique furniture gained more importance when seen against the strong yellow walls.

taking the outside edges first and then the centre. Take up all the excess and use your fingers to pleat this evenly. Repeat on the lower edge and handstitch the small pleats in place to secure.

STENCILLING THE CORNICE

The yellow paintwork was elegantly decorated with a black filigree stencil:

■ Trace out your image onto manilla card, then cut this out with a scalpel or craft knife. Hold the stencil card lightly on the cornice, using a little spray adhesive on the back. Spray with water-based craft paint (we used Gloss Black).

■ Hold the stencil flush against the cornice. To continue the repeat, mark the positions of the first stencil motif in chalk and line up the next motif accordingly. As you reposition the stencil, spray adhesive over the back to prevent paint from seeping under the card.

FINISHING TOUCHES

All Mary and Michael's original pieces of furniture and ceramics were carefully returned to the room, with just a few additions. The antique furniture made a far greater visual impact when viewed against the boldly painted yellow walls and the ceramic collections became even more prominent.

restful LIVING ROOM

Brad and Emily live in a ground floor flat that forms part of a row of Victorian terraces. Their living room was going to be redecorated by their neighbours Buster and Carol Anne and myself. The rooms have good-quality original wooden flooring and high ceilings. Large, double French doors open out onto the garden to give a bright, airy feel. The central feature of the room is a fireplace, complete with original mouldings which needed to be repainted in a colour more in keeping with the style. Carol Anne and Buster were also keen to reorganize the furniture and they desperately wanted to do something about the stack system supporting the TV and Hi-Fi. This was encouraging and my first suggestions got an enthusiastic response.

The sofa needed to be recovered but, with a budget of just £500, the only solution was to disguise it with a throw. The chaise longue, however, could be upholstered within the time and budget restrictions. Colour was important: the other rooms in the flat were all decorated in strong colours and so a contrasting softer palette would have more impact.

It was important to review the lighting as I wanted to create interesting pools of light in the corners of the room. I had a great ceiling height to work with and there was the potential to do something dramatic, but bearing in mind what other treatments were necessary, this called for some creative thinking!

Right: This photograph shows how the living room used to look before we totally transformed it (left). A Venetian mirror in the bedroom was exchanged for the heavy wooden one seen here.

GETTING STARTED

The warm, dappled finish of raw natural plaster was the inspiration for the wall finish. This colour is delicate but also very textural and an ideal background for the decorative effects that I wanted to use.

DESIGNER'S INSPIRATION BOARD

Pictures of crumbling fresco artworks inspired the decorative scheme. Earthy pigments and plaster finishes are perfect colours for interior decoration. By looking through holiday photographs and books on Italian architecture, I pulled together references for the paint effects and decoration. An ornate wall decoration was one of the strongest ideas: a classically-inspired acanthus leaf motif and bold calligraphy would certainly be a rather dramatic coupling with a plastery-pink palette of colour. The calligraphy was inspired by some engraved lettering on the foundation stones of an ancient Roman villa.

USE OF LIGHTING

The lighting in this room was extremely important. Softer pools of light introduced into the room by two floor lights made it more inviting. The large branch used for the central chandelier was found in a park and an electrician secured the five lighting cables from a ceiling rose through the suspended twig (see page 153).

When handling any electrical appliances, be sure to observe safety precautions at all times (see page 154). Do not allow twigs to come into contact with a naked light bulb.

Natural elements such as these seed pods, twigs and pebbles helped to inspire the design and decoration of the room.

CHECKLIST

DAY ONE:

• Prime and wax the fireplace
• Wash walls and woodwork
• Paint two base colours onto walls
• Apply photocopies to the walls
• Wash over the third paint colour
• Add the top coat of paint, plus finishing glaze

DAY TWO:

• Screw electric connector blocks to twiggy branch, remove centre light and hang chandelier
• Move chest and drill logs

• Finish waxing the fireplace
• Begin and complete calligraphy
• Rehang photographs
• Make side lamps from twigs and copper wire
• Decorate screens to hide TV and Hi-Fi
• Dye muslin drapes
• Move TV unit
• Paint curtain poles, reverse curtains and sew new headings into place
• Re-cover the chaise longue
• Make calico throw and cushions
• Hang antique Venetian mirror over fireplace

ANTIQUING THE FIREPLACE

The living room fireplace had some very beautiful details but the wax made them more noticeable. Coloured waxes, normally used as furniture polish, can be applied over an emulsion surface using a cloth or wire wool to add an instant patina of age and depth of colour.

■ To achieve this effect, sand the fireplace lightly at first using fine grade paper and then prime it with a coat of white acrylic primer. Make sure you cover the whole surface. Leave to dry for approximately one hour.

■ Finally, to complete the look, rub dark antiquing furniture wax across the surface using a pad of wire wool. Rub harder on the raised profiles to allow wax to build up in the recesses.

Far left: Candlesticks were fashioned from lengths of silver birch logs. A 2.5cm (1in) drill bit was used to bore a hole into the top of each log to a depth of 5cm (2in).

Left: A decorative detail of the fireplace.

FRESCO WALLS & CALLIGRAPHY

A rich wall treatment using a fresco finish, decoupage and calligraphy was paramount to the design at Belsize Park.

A FRESCO PAINT FINISH

The fresco effect is achieved by a gradual layering of emulsion colours and 10cm (4in) brushes are best for this technique. Colours can be blended whilst the paint is still wet so don't worry about drying times. The same brush can be used throughout the process.

■ Wash the walls and woodwork and then apply the two colours very patchily with the brush, pushing the paint out in all directions to build up an interesting textured surface.

DECOUPAGED LEAVES

Before the first colour was applied, enlarged photocopies of an acanthus leaf print were cut out and secured with border adhesive at intervals around the dado rail.

■ Use a dado rail as a positioning guide (or draw a horizontal line around your walls with a spirit level if they are plain) then use a retractable tape measure and tailor's chalk or a small piece of masking tape to assess the final positioning.

MATERIALS & EQUIPMENT

FRESCO FINISH
Paint kettle
Emulsion (Kohlrabi and Ivanhoe)
10cm (4in) brushes
Two small pots of Cameo Pink and Ginger Whip emulsion
Soft cloth
White emulsion
Scumble glaze

DECOUPAGE
Decoupage & calligraphy samples
Fine, sharp scissors

Spirit level (optional)
Retractable tape measure
Tailor's chalk or masking tape
Border adhesive

CALLIGRAPHY
Transparent acetate sheet
Overhead projector
Masking tape
Acrylic paint (Grey)
Saucer and fine artist's bristle brush
Clear acrylic varnish

■ Secure each copy onto the wall with border adhesive. Allow at least two hours for the glue to dry.

■ Complete the effect with a layer of colour. Mix two small pots of colour then thin with water, one part paint to four parts water. Wipe the paint over the walls with a damp cloth to build up areas of colour and to add interest.

■ Paint white emulsion (mixed in equal parts with scumble glaze) over the top.

Below: This acanthus leaf was enlarged from a copyright-free source-book to make a striking border at dado height around the room. When washed with thinned emulsion, it looks as though it has been painted by hand.

Above: The stunning fresco walls complete with calligraphy.

CREATING THE CALLIGRAPHY

To complete the wall finish, we transferred a wonderful poem about music onto the walls:

■ Photocopy your calligraphy onto a transparent acetate sheet or have this done for you at a photocopy bureau. Place the film onto an overhead projector. Once the image is aligned, secure with masking tape.

■ Thin some acrylic paint in an old saucer or jar. Using a fine artist's bristle brush, trace over the calligraphy projection. Aim to keep a sense of pattern and rhythm in the working style to capture the form of flowing script.

■ Every now and then switch off the projector to check the overall effect. Be careful not to jolt the machine otherwise the image may shift. When the paint is thoroughly dry, leave it to settle for at least an hour. Protect and seal with a coat of clear acrylic varnish and leave the calligraphy to dry thoroughly for at least two hours.

PUTTING THE LOOK TOGETHER

Twigs and leaves gathered from the garden were also bound around the floor lights. A vase of sculptural twisted willow echoed the graphic quality of the calligraphy.

A variety of different greens, used for both fabrics and accessories, balanced the softer, more earthy colours of the fireplace and walls. Bright acid-greens and softer pistachio shades were all combined to give the room a strong accent colour.

Small considerations, such as a branch of fresh mimosa and a bowl of bright green apples, added to the scheme.

TWIGGY FLOOR LIGHTS

Bunches of twigs were placed around the base of floor lamps, then bound with copper wire. Each shade was then decorated with dried leaves. To transform your own lights:

▩ Bind the twig ends tightly around the lamp base and secure with raffia. Snip the ends away neatly. Take a loop of copper wire and use pliers to twist this around the base. When secure, start to bind it upwards keeping it taut. Aim to keep each coil touching the previous one. Secure and trim away the excess.

▩ Press several leaves between the pages of a phone directory. Put weights on top and leave to dry for a week or two. Use a small dab of PVA glue to hold each leaf in place around the top edge of the shade. Bind a strand of raffia over the leaves. Knot this carefully and add a raffia bow, if appropriate. Secure with PVA glue.

MAKING THE SCREEN

Andy cut the TV unit to fit in better with the proportions of the room and a three-panelled screen was put together to hide the whole TV and Hi-Fi system (see pages 148–9). Decorate your own screen to echo the theme using the same technique as for the walls.

Above: The coloured glass containers were rather fortuitous finds in the kitchen. Cool green looked striking against the warmer muted fresco colour of the walls.

Right: The chaise longue was quickly re-covered and minimal stitching was required. I chose a different green to the shades used elsewhere in the room for a less contrived look.

WINDOW TREATMENT

Muslin sheers (dyed a deep green in the washing machine) were hung at the windows. These were stretched along old curtain wires and tied with heavy knots at the end. The curtains were hung on the reverse side (a buff-coloured lining) to pull together the natural look that was needed.

■ Strip the heading tape away, then fold the top raw edge over to meet the raw edge of the lining. Stitch a strip of hessian tape over the edges and sew ties along the length of this. Then rehang the curtains on the reverse side from repainted poles.

UPHOLSTERING THE CHAISE LONGUE

The chaise longue looked rather tired and needed a new look to go with the rest of the room:

■ Stretch a woven piece of fabric (we used Pistachio Green) over the seat base and then roughly trim to fit around the back rest. Turn the chaise longue on its side and staple the fabric to the frame keeping it taut at all times. Work from the centre of each side outwards. Fold the corners under neatly with a series of small tucks and then trim the excess away. Repeat for both the side arm rest and the back rest, tucking excess fabric into the sides.

■ To finish the curved arm section of the chaise longue, handstitch a shaped piece of fabric over the stapled edges. Recover the bolster and secure and disguise the gathered ends with a large, self-covered button.

FINISHING TOUCHES

Softness was brought into the room by draping a soft calico throw over the sofa. Finally, coordinating cushions were made up on a sewing machine.

loft BEDROOM

Even before we began work, the master bedroom in Steve and Alison's barn conversion was beautiful. The original barn had been an outbuilding that belonged to the farm where Alison and her sister Helen had grown up. They were a close family and obviously trusted one another to get on with the decorating, but just what did Rob and Helen have in mind for Steve and Alison?

Helen wanted to use bold greens or blues in the room and Rob suggested, 'Something to wake them up in the morning.' Helen wanted to get rid of the white walls and what she considered to be the clinical feeling. However, the look should definitely not be countrified. They were both sure of this and hated the patchwork quilt on the bed. I suggested some stencilling and by this, I meant not the teeny-weeny flowers round the door variety but something on a larger scale that looked like wrought iron. They liked the sound of this so I was on the right track.

There were a couple of things Helen pointed out, rather tactfully, that might not go down too well if they were painted or replaced. The overhead beams were original and had been painstakingly cleaned and waxed and there was also a rather huge glass Tiffany lightshade hanging from the central light fitting. The beams didn't worry me at all – I liked the rustic element – but the lightshade was a different story. It had taken Steve a whole weekend to put it up but his work was undone in minutes.

I felt uneasy about the original position of the bed (right) and when the time came to restyle the room, we all felt that the space was so much better organized (left).

GETTING STARTED

The proportions of the room were great but I wanted to organize it better by creating separate, functional areas.

DESIGNER'S INSPIRATION BOARD

I took inspiration for the colour simply by looking outwards onto the view. Beyond the garden swayed fabulous green fields of barley. Although it was a colour that was surprisingly difficult to find on regular paint charts, I had intended to mix my own colour from two chosen from a paint chart. One I thought was a little too strong and another too pale. Helen and Rob loved the bold colour (Mayan Green) before I had a chance to mix it. As soon as the paint hit the walls, I had to agree. It matched the barley fields outside perfectly.

I wanted to leave the paint as a solid block of colour on the walls without interrupting the intensity of this shade. The proportions of the room were so generous that I decided to paint a motif over the lower part of the walls, one that wouldn't interrupt the spaciousness in the room.

A huge stencil was used for both the bedcover and blinds and it needed a vibrant colour to add punchiness to the overall effect. Knowing that the chair covers would need a colour with good coverage to mask out the floral design, I used a strong magenta dye as my accent colour in the room.

When assembling the design board, almost by accident I introduced a touch of silver. This looked so great against the green and magenta that I decided to use quite a lot of silver-coloured accessories and I also gilded some MDF mirror frames in silver.

REVAMPING THE WOODWORK

The woodwork was painted using a soft creamy colour, while the beams and floorboards were left in their original colours:

▪ Sand the woodwork, then apply two coats of eggshell paint (we used Cloudy Amber Light). Leave to dry for an hour between coats.

PAINTING THE WALLS & CEILING

Very little preparation was needed to paint the walls. To carry out the same treatment on your walls:

▪ Tape dust sheets down, with plastic sheets underneath and cloth sheets on top. Apply at least two coats of paint (we used Mayan Green) with both long and short-handled rollers. When working with a high ceiling, use 'A' frame ladders with a wooden platform secured between the two frames. Cut in carefully around beams with a small brush.

DECORATING THE WALLS

We chose a twisting leaf motif from a copyright-free sourcebook and traced it around the wall just above the skirting board. The design was then painted in by hand using Spinach Green and a pointed, hard-bristled artist's brush. The hand finished quality contrasted well with the more graphic stencils in the room.

CHECKLIST

DAY ONE:
- Clear room
- Tape down dust sheets
- Paint woodwork
- Paint walls and ceiling
- Hand paint wall decoration
- Make up blinds and bedcover
- Stencil bedcover
- Make mirror frames and mosaic table
- Dye chair covers and curtain swag

DAY TWO:
- Stencil and hang blinds
- Make up screen
- Assemble chandelier
- Hang sails in roof space
- Gild and frame mirrors
- Make cushion covers

This swirling leaf motif was traced directly onto the wall just above the skirting board using an enlarged photocopy taken from a copyright-free sourcebook.

BLINDS & SCREENS

Large stencils have a bold, graphic quality. I was inspired by the wrought-iron bed and looked at images of iron grilles for source material to make my own stencil designs.

The blinds were hung from ceiling level right down to the low level windows. This makes the windows look much longer than they really are:

■ Make up Roman blinds (see pages 142–3). For the stencil, use an enlarged photocopy from a copyright-free book. Place this under masked-off glass, image

side up. Tape an acetate sheet over the glass and use a heat stencil cutter to 'draw' around the lines of your photocopy to cut the stencil.

■ Peel the stencil from the glass and spray adhesive onto the reverse. Lay the sheet over the top half of the blind, centring the image. Press the stencil over the blind. Dip a stencilling brush into black fabric paint and fill in the design. Leave to dry (about an hour), then press.

■ Fix the blinds onto a wooden batten screwed over the top of the window area. The batten is 10cm (4in) longer than the total width of three blinds. Use Velcro to secure each blind onto the batten. Cords from two blinds are pulled together from the left and one set are pulled from the right to raise and lower. Hold cords by cleats fixed to the wall.

■ Four dowelling pegs are fixed to the sides of and between each blind using double-ended screw fixings. The dowelling is cut with a jigsaw, sanded and then painted with matt black emulsion paint which dries in about an hour. Hang black tassels from the dowelling and twist 45cm (18in) width of dyed and knotted calico around each dowelling peg for a decorative swag.

STENCILLED BEDCOVER

The bedcover was sewn together using flat fabric panels of heavy cotton canvas:

■ Measure your own bed and cut canvas panels accordingly (add seam

MATERIALS & EQUIPMENT

BLINDS
Heavyweight canvas
Dressmaker's scissors
Retractable tape measure
Sewing machine and thread
Wooden batten (5 x 2.5cm/2 x 1in, total widths of three blinds plus 10cm/4in extra)
Velcro fastening
Long screws and rawlplugs
Power screwdriver
Blind cord rings (six for each blind)
Blind cord (about 10m/32ft for each blind)
Cleats (we used two)
4 x 25mm (1in) diameter dowelling in 10cm/4in lengths
Double-ended screw fixings
Jigsaw and medium-grade sandpaper

Matt emulsion paint (Black)
Black tasselled cords (1m/3ft long), one more than the number of blinds
Dyed calico fabric (Black), 45cm (18in) wide, width equal to total width of blinds plus about 50cm (20in)

STENCIL
Photocopier and copyright-free source material
Masking tape
Glass sheet (A1 size)
Acetate sheet
Heat stencil cutter (available from good stencil stores)
Adhesive spray
Large stencil brush and fabric paint (we used Black)

Left: The three stencilled blinds made a striking display, particularly when accessorized with a swag of magenta fabric and black tassels.

Below: The panelled screen had eight separate fabric panels. These were fixed to the frame using short curtain wires.

allowances of 2.5cm/1in). Sew and hem the edges. Stencil along the side flaps. Press to fix the fabric paint. Once dry, add piping.

SCREEN

Andy constructed a four panelled screen to hide an alcove area:

▆ Use butt joints (see page 150). For the horizontal timbers, use 7.5 x 2.5cm (3 x 1in) timber and the verticals need 5 x 2.5cm (2 x 1in) timber. The two tallest central panels are 150cm (5ft) high and two sides are 135cm (4½ft) high. All the panels measure 45cm (1½ft) across.

▆ Fix the horizontals between the verticals. Each vertical is drilled, countersunk and screwed using clamps and wood screws. Piano hinges link the panels and curtain wire holds the gathered drapes between panels (see page 63).

PUTTING THE LOOK TOGETHER

Seating was important as Steve and Alison would often sit and look at the view. Dry stone walling outside was echoed by a pebble mosaic table, while mirrors were gilded silver.

CREATING A CHANDELIER

Andy worked with us to construct a chandelier from MDF:

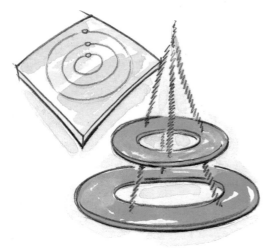

■ Cut two collars from 6mm (¼in) MDF (see pages 148–9). The diameter of the first collar is 90cm (36in) and 15cm (6in) wide and the second, smaller collar is 75cm (30in) in diameter and 12.5cm (5in) wide.

■ Cut six 30cm (12in) length chains (10mm/⅜in links) with wire cutters. Screw three cup hooks into the top of the smaller collar and hook the chains to the ceiling hook. Suspend the larger collar from three evenly-placed, centrally-positioned cup hooks fixed to the underside of the smaller collar.

■ Ask an electrician to split the electricity cable seven ways (three cables are 1m/3ft long and four are 1.5m/5ft long). Each cable ends with a pendant light fitting, over which an aluminium shade is fixed. Four cup hooks hold up the four lowest

lights and three cup hooks are used to hold the three highest ones. Secure each cable on the hook with cable clips.

CANVAS HANGINGS

The sail-shaped hangings are suitable for a beamed ceiling space:

■ Screw a cup hook into the beam at

the apex of the proposed sail. Then screw another into the lower position (our sails were positioned between two beams). Fix an eyelet into the top corner of the canvas with an eyelet fixer. Pass the eyelet through the apex cup hook and pull the fabric edge down towards the second hook. With the fabric pulled

A rather unconventional light fitting and long canvas sails were constructed to fill the vast ceiling space and to soften the dark coloured beams of the attic.

tight, fix an eyelet into it at the point of the cup hook. Decide the position of the third hook and screw it into the beam. Pull the fabric to this and hold taut.

■ Cut the fabric between the second and third hook. Fix an eyelet to where the third corner will stretch. Cut away excess fabric. Remove the sails and zigzag the raw edges, then sew down all three sides in a small hem before rehanging.

MAKING THE MIRRORS

Two silver mirrors (cut to size) were designed and cut from 6mm/¼in MDF:

■ Sketch templates onto pattern paper (the corners are identical so draw one). Trace onto MDF and jigsaw out.

■ Cut a rectangle to the mirror size out of the centre of the MDF. Gild the frames (we used silver aluminium leaf, see page 70). Secure MDF behind the mirror opening with panel adhesive and secure the mirror using more panel adhesive.

PEBBLE MOSAIC TABLE

Square or rectangular tables are suitable for this project:

■ Strip varnish, sand and apply white emulsion. When dry (one hour), distress with wire wool and clear beeswax.

■ Build the sides up using 2.5 x 1.3cm

(1 x ½in) timber screwed from underneath. Spread tile adhesive over the table surface and press pebbles into this. (Make sure none of the pebbles are above timber level.) Leave overnight, then secure toughened glass over the top with 'hockey stick' mouldings (from DIY stores) panel-pinned into position. Stain the pale wood (we used Burnt Sienna artist's colour). Leave for ten minutes and distress as before.

FINISHING TOUCHES

The chair covers were dyed Magenta and dyed calico was used to make cushions on the bed.

Two mirrors were made for the room. Silver aluminium leaf, as seen on this full-length mirror (above), is easy to apply. Finish off with a protective coat of varnish. The mirror is fixed in place with panel adhesive. Left: The completed pebble mosaic table reflects the walling outside the barn.

arts & crafts DINING ROOM

Michaela and David had struggled with decorating their dining room. The last painting spree was definitely it, they promised themselves and chose a bright, sunny yellow. However, once it left the paint pot, the sunny yellow became a rather sludgy and dirty-looking colour on the walls. The problem was simply the aspect of the room, advised Laurence Llewelyn-Bowen. North-facing rooms have a bluer, cooler light than rooms from a southern aspect that are filled with light. In addition to this, the room would be mainly used during the evening with artificial light, so the yellow stood little hope of survival.

The best way for an amateur decorator to select a paint is to test a patch on the walls first and to view the colours at different times of the day.

The early Victorian house would have been decorated with rich, deep colours and a room with this aspect may well have been decorated in blues or greens. Laurence chose Fern Green for the walls and took his inspiration from William Morris, one of the major figures of the Arts and Crafts Movement. Cathy and Mark, who worked with Laurence, felt that the look would be perfect for their friends' home. Encouraged by their enthusiasm, Laurence chose burgundy red fabric to help an expensive Morris fabric go further. Much to his delight, a quick inspection underneath the carpet revealed an original black and red tiled floor which convinced him that he was definitely on the right track.

Left: Now a far cry from the original room (right), Laurence carefully restored this dining room to its earlier Victorian origins, much to the delight of the owners.

GETTING STARTED Laurence encouraged Cathy and Mark to look back at an original scheme that would address the problems rather than to search for a contemporary, but too contrived, solution for the room.

DESIGNER'S INSPIRATION BOARD

William Morris established a style of textiles and interior design that was so strong that the original designs (and imitations) are still in production today. He had a real flair for decoration and designed carvings, metalwork, stained glass, furniture, ceramics, wallpapers and textiles that had a powerful impact on Victorian life.

Cathy's enthusiasm for Morris was a real bonus for Laurence: she loved the intricate patterns and rich, deep colours that are so often seen in his work. Laurence was able to use some William Morris-inspired fabric in the room and the flowing leaf patterns within the design inspired a drawing which he later translated into an intricate stencil. The fabric inspired not only the stencil motif but also the paint colour on the walls, the stencilling colours and the plain burgundy red fabric used for the curtains.

Laurence used lots of Michaela's furniture in the new design – a traditional pine dresser fitted in perfectly, together with her collection of gilt-edged plates. In addition to this, an absolute bargain was uncovered in Greenwich antique market – a beautifully detailed wooden overmantle that dominated the chimney breast and became a focal point.

The rich red tones and sage greens on this design board (left) were inspired by colours picked up from a sample of fabric and enhanced the warmth of the original flooring that was restored to its former glory (right).

PAINTING THE WALLS, BOARDING & CEILING

The colour used for the walls was Fern Green, a ready-mixed matt emulsion:

◼ Apply the paint as a flat colour using a roller fitted with a short-pile emulsion sleeve. (As the colour was so translucent, two coats were necessary, allowing an hour between coats.)

◼ One coat of Fern Green was also applied to the woodwork with 7.5cm (3in) brushes. This dries in an hour.

◼ Roughly paint the ceiling with matt emulsion and a brush (we used Chantilly for this and the frieze over the picture rail). Aim to build up a mottled effect with the paint.

RESTORING THE ORIGINAL FLOORING

Laurence discovered that the original flooring was still underneath the carpet. Only a small area in front of the chimney breast was missing (the site of the original hearth). The floor simply required a thorough clean. To clean tiles:

◼ Hire a floor polisher and use a mild solution of caustic soda (follow the manufacturer's instructions for this).

◼ Wipe the floor down with warm water, then buff with soft cloths and lots of liquid wax. Leave to dry for an hour.

STRIPPING THE TABLE

The dining room table was perfectly in keeping with the style but it needed to be stripped of varnish:

◼ Use chemical stripper to remove the layers of varnish with a scraper blade. Wash the surface with warm soapy water and protect with clear furniture wax applied with a soft cloth. Buff to a sheen after half an hour.

A collection of china was given pride of place as a display on the pine dresser.

CHECKLIST

DAY ONE:
- Clear room
- Roll-up old carpet
- Uncover original fireplace
- Paint walls, boarding and ceiling
- Clean floor tiles
- Fit frame for tiles
- Fit fireplace tiles
- Apply boarding to chimney breast
- Put up high shelf and mantle shelf

DAY TWO:
- Grout tiles
- Strip table
- Sew curtains and throw
- Cut stencil
- Stencil frieze
- Mount pictures in frames

PERIOD FIREPLACE

Laurence created a fireplace that would have been characteristic of the Victorian period from tongue-and-groove boarding, a high shelf, mantle shelf and tiling.

Laurence's first task was to form a neat hole around the original firestone back:

■ Use a hammer to tap away at the centre of the chimney breast until you hear a hollow sound. Continue to tap until the covering breaks and the void is uncovered. Straighten up untidy edges with sand and cement, then smooth away with a trowel.

MATERIALS & EQUIPMENT

Small hammer
Sand and cement mix
Trowel
Bevelled wood (enough to go around the architrave area)
Paper and pencil
Retractable tape measure
Spirit level
Mitre block
Panel adhesive
Long, flat-headed nails
All-purpose filler and filler knife

Tongue-and-groove boarding (enough to cover a chimney breast)
Power saw
MDF for brackets and shelves (we used widths of 6mm/¼in and 2.5cm (½in) and lengths of 5sq m/17sq ft)
Rawlplugs
Long wood screws (7.5cm/3in)
Power drill and power screwdriver
Medium-grade sandpaper
Jigsaw
Ceramic tiles
Claw hammer

Right: The focal point of the new room was the fireplace. Although it was actually unsuitable for a real fire, stacked logs helped to create the illusion of one.

■ Fit an architrave frame around the opening for the tiles. (Measure the area roughly before opening and allow a few extra tiles.) Use a long spirit level to ensure that the sides and angles are square. Lay the tiles (see opposite) against the wall to determine the architrave shape and follow the proportions of the opening.

■ Mitre the architrave corners (see page 149). Use panel adhesive to secure this to the wall. Hammer flat-headed nails halfway into the wall to hold the architrave whilst the adhesive sets firmly.

■ Fit boarding around the chimney breast with panel adhesive. The first board fits into the corner of the chimney breast with the tongue of the board facing inwards. Press firmly in place and hold for 30 seconds. Tap a long, flat-headed nail partially into the wall through the top, bottom and middle of the board to hold until the adhesive sets firmly (about two hours). Continue for the other boards, cutting the timber close to the architrave edge and skirting.

■ Cut four corner brackets with a power saw from MDF (we used 6mm/¼in) from a paper outline. (Our outline was made from a curved shape with a right angle at the top edge to fit against the wall.) Mark the positions on the boarding, then screw the brackets into the wall with long wood screws. Pre-drill holes through the narrow edge of each bracket and countersink. Fill the holes with filler and sand when dry (about 20 minutes).

■ To make a deep shelf, take three pieces of MDF sawn from 2.5cm (½in) MDF into 20cm (8in) wide strips using a jigsaw. Place the strips onto the brackets and screw into the timber across the top of the boards.

■ Make the mantle shelf in a similar way to the high shelf. Cut two more brackets following the original template and secure into the wall in the same way. Cut a slightly narrower shelf from MDF with a jigsaw. This time the fixing screws need to go through the top of the shelf into the narrow edge of the bracket. Remove the nails from the boarding with a claw hammer.

■ To add the high shelf, screw three pieces of pre-drilled timber (ours were 2.5 x 2.5cm/1 x 1in) above the boarding around the chimney breast.

The architrave determines the space that needs to be tiled. Use a notched tile adhesive spreader to apply a layer of white ready-mixed filling adhesive all over the area to be tiled. Press the top left-hand tile squarely into the corner. Add the next tile, and so on, applying spacers between each tile until you have covered the area. Leave to dry thoroughly overnight before you begin grouting (see page 153).

PUTTING THE LOOK TOGETHER

A detailed frieze created from stencilling drew together all the elements that went into achieving the finished William Morris look.

■ Stitch border strips around three sides of a lining fabric width. (The length of the curtain is the drop from curtain rail to floor plus 5cm/2in for turnings.)

■ To make the pelmet, iron a strip of fabric onto a pre-cut length of iron-on buckram (pelmet stiffener). Fold the raw edges to the wrong side. Use Velcro to attach the fabric to the pelmet which is made from a piece of 5 x 2.5cm (2 x 1in) battening fixed above the curtain track (see page 152).

ITALIAN STRUNG CURTAINS

The fabric coverings that hung over both the door and window were strung with blind cords to create diagonally shaped drapes. We used a width of burgundy fabric onto which three border strips (15cm/6in) of William Morris fabric were stitched. Hem the outside edge using a small 2.5cm (1in) seam.

Laurence discovered a clock (right) in the loft. Michaela had bought it on holiday and it fitted in perfectly with the arts and crafts theme of the completed William Morris room (above).

■ View the curtains looking downwards when they are hung from ceiling to floor to string the curtains correctly. Hold the edge of the curtain approximately one third of the way up from the floor. Gather this upwards along the diagonal into the top right-hand corner, allowing the folds to curve.

■ Whilst holding the curtain tightly, use safety pins to catch the folds at the back along the diagonal (one pin every 10cm/4in) and pass each pin through both fabric thicknesses.

■ Fasten blind rings to the pins and thread with nylon cord starting at the lowest point, working upwards to the top right-hand corner. Pass the cord through an eyelet screwed into the pelmet batten then pass down the outer edge and secure on a cleat. Then check the workings.

■ Remove the safety pins and sew each ring securely onto the blind, stitching through both fabrics. Repeat for the adjacent curtain.

DESIGNING THE STENCIL FRIEZE

The stencil frieze was applied over a painted border of cream-coloured emulsion (we used Chantilly). A picture rail divided the green and cream. Laurence used matchpots (terracotta and green) together with the same colour as the walls. He made a Morris-inspired stencil:

■ Lay your design over oiled manilla card, securing carbon paper underneath. Trace around the outline with a pencil.

■ Lift off the artwork and carbon paper to reveal the image. Using a cutting mat, cut out the design with a craft knife.

■ Use a dry stencil brush and stippling motion to stencil in the design.

FINISHING TOUCHES

The room was styled with embroidery designs that Laurence's great aunt had painted. He framed Cathy and Mark's own pictures and also added a dried flower garland. A traditional pair of metal candle sconces were fixed onto the wall and the over-mantle mirror (found in a local market) was placed directly over the fireplace.

The throw was made up from a piece of William Morris-style fabric and cushions were added to complete the look.

Above: Stencils such as this one are easy to cut and, as seen here, dark colours set against a cream background are most effective.

Below: A symmetrical arrangement is an effective way of displaying small pictures or prints.

multi-purpose GUEST ROOM

Mark and Cathy's spare room needed some loving care and attention. Since moving in, they had done very little to the room apart from painting it in red-and-white stripes. The sink was never used, the beds were old and storage was a big problem. The room was generally used as a playroom although it also stored a computer.

Anna Ryder Richardson was confident that the room could function in several different ways. One use was as a spare bedroom. However, the room could also be somewhere for the children to play and why not also accommodate a smart office space? Michaela and David, their friends and neighbours, were impressed with Anna's ideas but how could they hope to achieve all this in two days?

There were a few features in the room that Anna could work with but no cupboard or storage areas. The room was used so infrequently as a spare room that it was decided that the two beds should be replaced with a sofa bed. Anna's initial plan was to remove everything from the room and to assess the space. A bay window allowed plenty of natural light into the room and there was also a Victorian fireplace. Basically, the room was an open space that Anna and her team looked forward to reinventing.

Our 'before' picture (right) shows that this room needed a rethink. It was redecorated and carefully planned and reorganized to accommodate plenty of storage space.

GETTING STARTED

This multi-purpose room needed to be unified so Anna decided to use a lively citrus colour scheme to bring all the elements together.

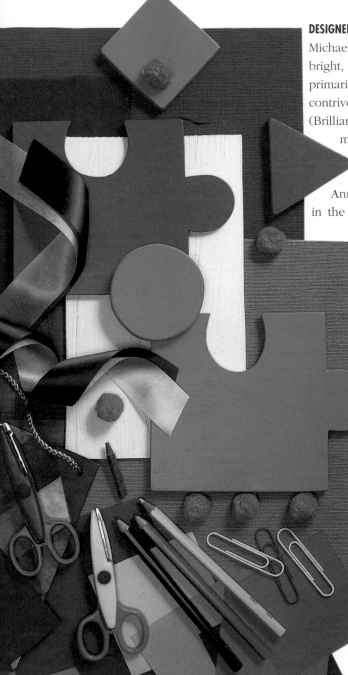

DESIGNER'S INSPIRATION BOARD

Michaela and David suggested that they should work with bright, jazzy colours that would appeal to children. Bold primaries were an obvious choice but seemed a little contrived so they chose to use a palette of burnt orange (Brilliant Tangerine) and a lime green (Spicy Green) for the majority of the paintwork. Softer shades of lemon and lime would be used on the walls to highlight the puzzle shapes on the storage cupboards.

Anna had plans for alternate jigsaw shapes to be painted in the orange and lime colours to build up a giant jigsaw puzzle effect. These colours were also combined to make cushions, shelves and a throw.

A corner of the room was used to build a combined seat and bench, the top of which could be lifted up to reveal a generous storage area. An alcove was used for a low-level double-fronted cupboard. Alongside the work area, a three-tiered cupboard was built, once again using the intersecting puzzle shapes for all the doors.

Anna wanted to emphasize the shape of the bay windows, yet still have the flexibility to shut out the light when the room was used as a bedroom and to filter it during the day. Coloured roller blinds were hung at the top of the windows so that they could be pulled halfway down during the day or completely down at night. Coloured, sheer café-style curtains screened the lower half of the windows. Privacy was then maintained, yet the natural light could still be enjoyed. The blocks of colour created by the combination of both blinds and curtains fitted in well with the strong puzzle theme.

Elementary puzzle shapes in bold colours set the theme for the room. Other colours were used elsewhere in the space but on a smaller scale.

PREPARING THE ROOM

The room was cleared, the carpet and underlay were rolled up and removed, and gripper rods were taken out using a claw hammer. The sink was ripped out and old pipes were disconnected (a qualified plumber will do this for you). Several of the original floorboards were missing and Andy replaced these with sections cut from a length of floorboard:
▨ Measure the width of the old floorboards and buy new ones to match. Cut each board using a power jigsaw to fit the space and nail them onto the underlying floor joists with long nails.

SANDING THE FLOORBOARDS

While Andy started work on the puzzle doors, Anna began sanding the floorboards (see pages 130–1). The floor was protected with lime wax:
▨ Rub the wax into the floor as though you were polishing shoes. Work along one floorboard at a time to achieve an uneven, patchy finish. Once covered, buff up with soft cloths.

PAINTING THE CEILING, WALLS & WOODWORK

All these items were painted in a pale colour (Lemon Whip) to define the stronger-coloured furniture and accessories in the room:
▨ Roller-paint the walls and ceiling with matt emulsion applied with a 7.5cm (3in) brush. With the same brush, apply a contrasting colour above picture rails (we used New Green matt emulsion).
▨ Paint the skirtings and doors using an eggshell finish (Lemon Whip). Use a 7.5cm (3in) brush for filling in and cut in with a 2.5cm (1in) brush. Then paint the picture rail in an eggshell finish (Spicy Green) with a 2.5cm (1in) brush and leave to dry for two hours.

CHECKLIST

DAY ONE:
- Disconnect old sink
- Sand and lime-wax floor
- Paint ceiling, walls, doors and woodwork
- Prepare MDF shapes for cupboards
- Construct cupboard structures
- Make storage/seating area

DAY TWO:
- Make desk area
- Sew cushions and bean bags
- Make and hang roller blinds
- Sew and hang sheer curtains
- Make firescreen and throw
- Fix metal hanging rack
- Put up shelves

▨ Leave the paints to dry thoroughly overnight. (Emulsion paint touch-dries in about an hour while eggshell paints which are oil-based require at least two hours for drying.)

Andy's carpentry skills were put to good use when constructing this unique three-tier 'jigsaw puzzle' cupboard.

WORK AREA & COLOURFUL CUPBOARDS

The main problem here was storage. With cupboards to hold everything, the room would work more efficiently. Anna designed some cupboard doors in the shape of jigsaw pieces.

Geometric shapes were cut from MDF for the handles, then dowelling was screwed through the wood to secure them.

CUPBOARDS

Andy made a three-tier cupboard from a timber framework and shaped the sides:

■ Fix two vertical lengths of 5 x 5cm (2 x 2in) timber onto the 'L' shaped corner of the wall at the outside edges of the proposed unit. Make two rectangular timber frames. Each frame is constructed from three widths of 5 x 5cm (2 x 2in) timber (one piece at the top, one at the bottom and one in the centre) and two vertical pieces of timber are cut to the desired height of the cupboard.

■ Position the frames against the timbers screwed to the wall to make the box-shaped framework for the cupboard. Screw the frames into the wall timberwork, through the floorboards and to each other.

■ Measure the frame for the cupboard doors and cut one piece of MDF. Mark on the three jigsaw shapes and cut these out. Hinge each door onto the framework. Face the second side with MDF and cut two shelves and a top for the inside of the cupboard. Secure each shelf to the framework with fixing blocks and face one side with MDF. Paint and seal with varnish.

STORAGE/SEATING BENCH

Andy constructed a multi-purpose storage bench. To make your own:

■ Measure out the required width and height of the bench and mark this directly onto the wall. Screw two lengths of 5 x 5cm (2 x 2in) timber horizontally

MATERIALS & EQUIPMENT

Retractable tape measure
Jigsaw
Spirit level
Wood drill and masonry bits
Countersink and power drill
Pencil
Power screwdriver
Rawlplugs and long and short screws
6mm (¼in) MDF
Wood glue
Hand plane
Ready-mixed filler
Paint, as required (we used Brilliant
  Tangerine and Spicy Green)
7.5cm (3in) brushes

Acrylic varnish
Flush hinges

CUPBOARDS
5 x 5cm (2 x 2in) timber
Lining paper
Scissors
5cm (2in) dowelling

BENCH
5 x 5cm (2 x 2in) timber
5 x 2.5cm (2 x 1in) timber battens

DESK
5 x 2.5cm (2 x 1in) timber battens
5 x 5cm (2 x 2in) timber

An angled desk was made by fixing a 5 x 2.5cm (2 x 1in) batten to the wall at the required height for the back. The top was cut from MDF. Rest the top against the batten and ask another person to hold two lengths of 5 x 5cm (2 x 2in) timber at a slight angle to the front edge of the MDF. Mark the angle against the timber and trim with a jigsaw. Screw legs onto the top through predrilled holes and screw the top into the wall batten. Fill holes and paint and varnish the desk.

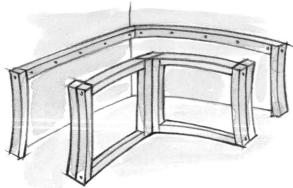

onto the 'L' shaped corner of the wall at the desired bench height. Predrill and countersink holes 4cm (1.5in) from each end. Using a spirit level, hold the longest batten against the wall at the required height and screw the batten to the wall.

■ Make an 'L' shaped timber framework for the front of the bench that will support the MDF. Saw five vertical pieces of 5 x 5cm (2 x 2in) timber at the height of the bench and screw 5 x 2.5cm (2 x 1in) timber through three of the verticals to make an 'L' shaped frame. Screw the frame in place through the floorboards and screw the other two verticals onto the wall at either end of the bench.

■ Face the timber framework with pieces of MDF, countersink holes and screw in place. Cut two pieces of MDF for the backrest and fix these against the wall with panel adhesive. Finally, cut the lid from two pieces of MDF (for two storage areas) and hinge to the frame- work with flush hinges. Paint the bench in the same citrus colours as the rest of the furniture and apply a coat of varnish to seal and protect the surface.

PUTTING THE LOOK TOGETHER

The harlequin combination of colours was the dominant theme of this room and the mix of colours followed through on most of the accessories and soft furnishings.

Cotton pompom fringing is easy to dye using a small pot of cold water dye. It really helps to lift these envelope cushions.

COORDINATING CUSHIONS

Cushions were made from a coordinating fabric:

■ For the pompon cushions, cut the front including a 2.5cm (1in) seam allowance. Cut a second piece to the same width as the front, but the length should be one-and-three-quarters the length of the front. Cut in half across its length. Turn the edges under each side of the horizontal cut.

■ Lay the cushion front right side up and lay bobbled trim around the sides, keeping the pompoms towards the centres. Baste in place. Lay the front

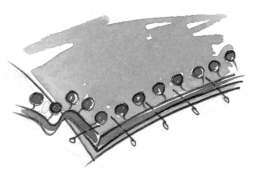

and back pieces, right sides together and raw edges even. Stitch around the sides and turn to the right side. Fill with a pad. Hem the overlapping back piece.

■ For round cushions, use a plate to cut fabric. Pin, tack and sew a 7.5cm (3in) border. Insert trimming into the seam at the same time, with the pompoms facing inwards. Leave a turning gap, add a pad and sew to close.

BRIGHT BEAN BAGS

The bean bags were really easy to make:

■ Cut six squares of fabric (about 61cm/24in square), four from one colour and two from a second colour. With right sides together and raw edges even, sew four squares together to create a row of four squares. Sew the two outside edges together to create an open-ended box shape.

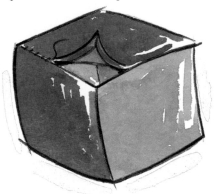

■ Sew the two remaining squares onto the box shape to close, leaving a small turning gap. Fill with polystyrene bean bag balls and then stitch the gap securely to close.

MULTI-COLOURED ROLLER BLINDS

Use hessian cotton fabric and a roller blind kit to make the colourful blinds:

■ Measure the width and required drop, adding 5cm (2in) to the bottom hem and cut out the fabric. Hem all four sides with a close zigzag on the sewing machine with matching cotton.

■ Turn over and hem the bottom edge to make a small pocket. Slide the

The windows were made to look more interesting with roller blinds (left) fitted at the top and sheer café curtains below. The bold panels of colour contrasted well with the rest of the room. A brightly coloured fireguard (below) was made by weaving lengths of ribbon across a timber frame. Small tacks hold the ribbons securely at the edges. Although the fireguard is fine for decorative purposes, it should never be placed in front of an open fire.

wooden batten (supplied in kits) into this. If necessary, trim the batten with a tenon saw. Place the top of the fabric over the round dowelling supplied for the top of the blind. Staple or tack in place, working from the ends to the centre. Hang the blind in position and fix a cleat two-thirds of the way down the architrave to hold the cords.

CAFÉ CURTAINS

Sheer café curtains were made up from vibrantly coloured fabrics:
- Measure the window width, add another half width, then measure the curtain drop. Cut out fabric, adding 2.5cm (1in) for turnings. Zigzag raw edges on a sewing machine and hem.
- Fold back the top hem and sew close to the raw edge to create a channel for the curtain wire. Cut the wire to the width of the window less one-tenth. Pass the wire through the curtain top and gather up the excess fabric. Fix rings onto the wires and screw hooks into the architrave. Pull the wire taut to hang the curtains on the hooks.

FINISHING TOUCHES

Two beaded throws were hand-stitched together down the centre to make a sofa throw and a boldly coloured rug softened the floorboards. Finally, Anna accessorized the room with toys and fixed a metal hanging rack and shelves (see page 151) in the office area.

feng shui BEDROOM

Anne had surprised and delighted Laurence Llewelyn-Bowen, the designer working on the room, when she had said to him that she was sure that dark khaki green was 'just the colour' for her friends' bedroom. It's not often that we meet such emphatic colourists on our programme. David, Anne's partner, suggested that the room should be given a touch of old-fashioned colonial style and this seemed to fit in quite well with Anne's ideas. The overall scheme developed quickly from the first meeting. It was a strong and dramatic brief.

The room was well proportioned and although it was not generous in size, there was space at either side of the double bed and room at the end for storage drawers, a small table and a chair. However, the main problem for Laurence to solve was that there was no wardrobe. Debra and Colin had been using a hanging rail. It held all their clothes but in a very 'undesigner-ish' sort of way and it would have to go. In such a small room it was difficult to decide exactly where a double wardrobe could be fitted.

Two small windows allowed enough daylight into the room for it to be fairly bright, but a lighting scheme still needed to be included as dark green absorbs a lot of light. The flooring also needed to be reviewed. It was evident that there would have to be a few compromises made along the way in order to keep within the strict budget.

Left: Laurence left the bed in its original position (right) but added some colonial style muslin drapes at either side of the bed to match up with the curtains at the windows.

GETTING STARTED

Khaki green seemed to offer a very small palette but, in fact, the colours ranged from dusty green beiges to intense pond-like greens and Laurence finally settled on a rich shade of olive green.

DESIGNER'S INSPIRATION BOARD

Laurence wanted to introduce the practice of Feng Shui into the room. Pronounced 'Fung Shoy', this is an ancient Chinese philosophy from 4,000 years ago. It is a deeply complex study concerning the art of living harmoniously with your environment to achieve health, wealth and happiness. Developing good energy channels at home can improve your living standards and good fortune. The cardinal rule is that there must be a balance in the room. Light surfaces are balanced with darker; matt against shiny or smooth against rough so that the end result is visually pleasing. Laurence chose a dark matt olive green colour for the walls and ceiling with reflective copper leaf and textured artex for decoration. The wardrobe ran from floor to ceiling. When it was painted in the same colour as the walls, it seemed to disappear. Even the copper leaf handles blended in with the wall decorations.

CREATING THE TIMBER FLOOR BORDER

The first task was to lay timber strips around the sides of the room to enclose some navy blue carpeting:

■ Fix 15cm (6in) planks in place using panel adhesive applied over the chipboard.

■ Tap flat-headed nails in place every 60cm (24in) with a hammer. (Remove these when the adhesive is set.) Use the longest uninterrupted wall to position the first board, then fit the others.

■ Cut out notches of timber when fitting around radiator

Laurence's design board was inspired by the art of Feng Shui (left). The pine floorboards (right) were used to enclose a rich blue carpet remnant.

pipes and other awkward areas with a jigsaw. Mitre corners with a rotary saw.

■ Apply acrylic floor varnish with a 10cm (4in) brush. Leave for one hour.

REORGANIZING THE LIGHTING

An electrician separated one of the light cables in the loft space into four. Each cable was taken into a corner of the room and a ceiling rose was fitted.

CONSTRUCTING THE WARDROBE

Andy made the wardrobe structure using a 5 x 2.5cm (2 x 1in) timber framework:

■ Measure the available width, length and height to decide the size of your wardrobe. (We built a rectangular framework using 5 x 2.5cm/2 x 1in timber.)

■ Use long screws to fix the timber on one side of the wall, across the ceiling and against the floor.

■ Fix the MDF doors and side section to the frame with countersunk screws and kitchen hinges. For the handles, cut two pieces of 10cm (4in) square MDF and secure onto square timber blocks of exactly the same size (2.5cm/1in deep). Secure the handles from the inside of the doors with small screws.

■ Fill holes with all-purpose filler and

CHECKLIST

DAY ONE:

- Clear room
- Measure, cut and secure floor timber
- Re-route light and fix electric cables
- Construct wardrobe
- Dye string, apply copper spray to clay and thread piping and nuggets
- Stipple artex squares onto walls
- Paint walls, ceiling, skirting and radiators with dark green emulsion

DAY TWO:

- Fix carpet remnant on floor
- Fix new wardrobe handles in position
- Bend copper piping and fix around bed and above window area
- Apply copper leaf panels to artex
- Stencil squares onto bedlinen
- Spray light flex copper
- Paint bamboo roller blinds
- Hang blinds, window and bed sheers
- Hang new lights

leave this to dry for ten minutes. Use acrylic gold size on the handles, wait until tacky, then press copper leaf on top. Remove the backing paper and protect with spray varnish. Leave to dry for about an hour.

The wardrobe, with its clever copper handles, is almost invisible and four low lights, placed in corners of the room, add soft pools of light.

COPPER CONTRASTS & COOL DRAPES

Copper highlights were used to great effect at key points on the walls, accessories and fabrics. Contrasts of texture, as well as colour, also played an important part in this room.

Bamboo roller blinds were sprayed with car paint and re-hung, then delicate muslin drapes were added.

Shiny copper curtain poles held muslin drapes and these contrasted perfectly against the dark green walls. The drapes were decorated with tiebacks made from string and copper beads.

■ To determine the length of the pole, take a piece of string and follow the proposed shape of the rail on the wall. Hold the piping steady on a workbench and cut off the required length squarely.

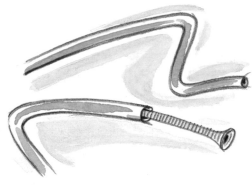

■ Use a plumber's pipe bender to create the unusual bends. Insert it into the piping and bend at a point where the bracket would be fixed into a 90-degree angle. Repeat the procedure closer to the end of the pipe, bending it back in the other direction to produce an 'S' shape and repeat at the other end.

■ Each curtain is made from a single width of sheer cotton muslin. The drop was the floor to ceiling measurement plus 20cm (8in) extra for hems and to allow for a generous bunching up at floor level. Cut the fabric and press.

■ Fold the hem over (2.5cm/1in) and sew to close the turned edge using a running stitch. Fold a similar double hem at the top of the curtain, allowing a 5cm (2in) hem. Sew as before.

■ Pass the copper rail through the channel produced at the top hem of the

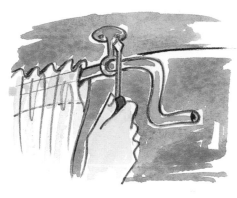

fabric. Drill and rawlplug fixing holes and screw copper brackets to the ceiling above the window. Hang the rails from the brackets.

MATERIALS & EQUIPMENT
CURTAIN POLES
String
15mm (¾in) thick copper piping
Hacksaw
Plumber's pipe bender
Copper piping brackets (2 for each rail)
Power drill and masonry bit
Rawlplugs
Small hammer (to tap in rawlplugs)
Copper screws (2 for each bracket)
Small and power screwdriver

MUSLIN CURTAINS
White muslin
Dressmaker's scissors
Sewing machine
Rough sisal string
Handwash dye (we used Black)
Small block of air-dried clay
Aerosol spray paint (we used Copper)
Needle and matching thread
Spray lacquer or varnish
Hooks (for tiebacks)

The elegant bed drapes were held back with loops of dyed black string.

Cut pieces of string to the required lengths and dye using a cold handwash fabric dye according to the manufacturer's instructions. Leave in the airing cupboard to dry or speed up the process with a hairdryer

Form the end beads from clay. (The clay air-dries in about four hours.) Spray the clay beads with aerosol spray. Thread one bead onto the end of a knotted length of string, then thread a 5cm (2in) piece of copper pipe over the bead. Lacquer or varnish and sew the string onto the curtain top. Add hooks and tiebacks made from dyed string.

To hold the bed drapes, Laurence fixed brackets to the ceiling above the bed (two on each side) and suspended rails from these.

PUTTING THE LOOK TOGETHER

The main focus of the room was the combination of different surfaces, textures and colour. For Laurence, it was balancing the yin and yang forces of the room.

CREATING TEXTURED WALLS

Artex squares introduced a textured surface against the flat colour of the paint. To carry out the same treatment:

■ Work out the number of artex squares that you wish to apply along one wall and the width of each square. Subtract the total width of the squares from the wall measurement and divide the remainder by the number of squares plus one. This measurement equals the width of each gap between the squares.

■ Determine the size and position of each square using a tape measure, ruler and spirit level around the walls. Use the spirit level to keep the lines square and mark each square in pencil.

■ Mask the squared-off areas from the surrounding wall using masking tape. The centre of each of our squares was also masked off to the same size as a square of copper leaf.

■ Apply artex with a small brush. Remove the masking tape and leave to dry for at least two hours.

DECORATING THE WALLS & OTHER SURFACES

Once the artex was dry, the walls, ceiling, skirting and radiators were painted with emulsion (we used an olive green) applied with a roller and cut in with a 5cm (2in) brush.

■ The emulsion on the walls will dry in about an hour but you will need to apply two coats to the artexed areas. Mask off the artexed areas and, with a small roller, apply an emulsion paint (we used Royal Blue) to the area.

■ Once dry, paint acrylic gold size onto the area. Leave until tacky and then press copper leaf over the glue. Use the backing paper to smooth the leaf carefully over the surface.

■ Pull away the backing paper. Leave for an hour, protect the leaf with spray varnish, then remove the masking tape.

COLONIAL-STYLE BEDDING

Copper squares were painted directly onto the duvet cover:

■ Mark the positions of the squares onto the cover in pencil. (Use a retractable tape measure to align accurately and mask off with regular masking tape.)

■ Slide a plastic bag between the duvet cover so as not to let the colour bleed through, then apply fabric paint (we used Copper) to colour each square

Below: Copper leaf and gold size is applied over blue emulsion. Gaps in the leaf reveal traces of blue colour.

Reflective copper leaf squares on the walls (right and above) matched painted copper squares that were stencilled onto the bedcover using copper-coloured fabric paint.

using a 5cm (2in) brush. Press on the reverse side with a warm iron when dry (about an hour) to fix the colour.

FINISHING TOUCHES

Styling was kept to a minimum to allow the positive flow of Chi energy to flow around the room. Exotic orchids emphasized the colonial aspect and the copper was brilliantly reflective against the matt walls. The electric flex for the dropped corner lights was sprayed copper and shades (with copper insides) were hung from pendants.

Finally, the blinds were sprayed black with car paint and rehung. Coordinating cushion covers completed the look.

gothic BEDROOM

As Liz Wagstaff made her way to the top bedroom in the house on the Isle of Dogs, she was beginning to formulate ideas. Anne and David, the owners, had been punks in their earlier days and the house was testament to their love of the unusual and often bizarre. Heavy black ash furniture decorated most of the rooms, including a black ash goldfish tank in the living room. Liz couldn't help but notice the vibrant blue and yellow rag-rolled walls in the living room too – these were people who weren't afraid to experiment with colour.

Debra and Colin, the neighbours who were working with Liz in the bedroom, had definite ideas about what they wanted to do to their friends' room. Gothic was the overriding theme – 'Think of *Interview with the Vampire* and you've got it.' They wanted blood red and purple walls, with a touch of Dracula too.

A lack of wardrobe space was Liz's main concern as Anne and David had a clothes collection that the V & A museum would be proud to own. The furniture in the room was black ash, including two bedside tables, a large chest of drawers and a mirror.

The Gothic look was Liz's starting point, but she felt that red and purple colours might be too dominant. A stone effect would make a good background and stronger colours could be used elsewhere. This sounded enough like Dracula's castle for Debra and Colin.

The black ash furniture units (right) were relics from Anne and David's earlier years but Liz brought them up-to-date with her artful paintwork and decoupage (left).

GETTING STARTED

Once Liz had convinced both Debra and Colin that the stone-effect wall would work well, they had to decide where to use intense purples and reds in the room.

DESIGNER'S INSPIRATION BOARD

Liz watched the film *Interview with the Vampire* following a recommendation from Debra and Colin. Gargoyles are *de rigueur* in any horror movie and Liz was keen to line the walls with them.

Liz discovered a copyright-free sourcebook on historical ornament and design. She found examples of Gothic architecture, most notably the arch that was used as a border around the chest of drawers. She also used her knowledge of Horace Walpole's Strawberry Hill house to plan out her scheme. The rich creams, used with golds and reds, came from this source as did the shaped pelmets.

Liz also had the Houses of Parliament practically on her doorstep and she studied some of the details executed by the architect Pugin, who was a key figure in the revival and development of the Gothic style, in this beautiful building.

PAINTING THE WALLS & RADIATOR

The ceiling and skirting were left in their original cream and the first task was to paint the stone-effect walls. As the white paint on the walls provided a good base, Liz applied scumble glaze directly over the top of this:

■ Mix up tinted scumble glaze using six parts acrylic glaze to one part

Liz's design board (left) shows an intriguing collection of ideas for the Gothic look. Plaster gargoyles (right) were brushed with the same scumble glaze as the walls. The still-wet glaze was then rubbed with a cloth to highlight raised parts of the faces.

coloured emulsion (we used Gobi Tan).

▦ Use a 10cm (4in) brush to apply the glaze directly onto the wall. Brush outwards to build up a cloudy effect.

▦ While the glaze is wet, go back over the painted area with a soft cloth. Rub the surface lightly to remove brushmarks and to blur hard edges. Work one section at a time, first brushing on the glaze and then wiping the surface with the cloth. Leave to dry for one hour.

CREATING THE PAPER FRIEZE

Liz photocopied details from a copyright-free sourcebook to make a paper frieze:

▦ Tape your enlarged motifs together on the reverse and photocopy enough times to run around your walls.

▦ Tint the photocopies with a solution of one part water-based ink (we used sepia) with one part water. Brush ink over the copies using a 5cm (2in) brush and leave to dry for one hour.

▦ Cut the frieze from the paper and secure to the walls using PVA adhesive. (Mark the appropriate height round the walls with a tape measure and a pencil.)

▦ Brush PVA glue over the back of the frieze using a 5cm (2in) brush and press the frieze onto the walls. Brush the copies flat with a brush coated in PVA.

▦ Mix up a tinted scumble glaze (four parts glaze to one part Magnolia matt emulsion). Lightly brush this over the ink and leave to dry for 30 minutes.

PAINTED FLOORCLOTH

Liz used cotton duck canvas as a floor cloth. To make your own:

▦ Cut the canvas to size and pre-wash it to remove any finishing treatments. Press the reverse of the damp canvas with a hot iron and leave to dry. Hem the raw edges down at the back.

CHECKLIST

DAY ONE:
- Clear room
- Base-coat walls with Magnolia
- Paint stone effect on walls and tables
- Glaze and fix gargoyles to walls
- Cut out and tint decoupage borders
- Paste-up border
- Cut MDF shapes to fit over doors
- Make bedhead and corona

DAY TWO:
- Make floor cloth
- Paint and decorate doors

- Fix wardrobe pelmet into place, create tassels and hang drapes
- Sew curtains
- Fix curtain poles and hang curtains
- Sew and hang muslin sheers
- Stitch wardrobe fabric panels
- Paint and decoupage the chest of drawers and mirror
- Change light fitting
- Sew bedspread
- Make up cushions
- Decorate lampshades

▦ Paint the canvas with emulsion (we used Princess Blue) and then seal and protect the surface with a coat of acrylic varnish, which dries in approximately one to two hours.

Tassels were made from corrugated cardboard, then gilded and strung onto gold cord to complete the curtains.

GOTHIC ARCHES

The Gothic arch shape was used in several ways around the room, the fretwork bedhead being perhaps the most dramatic project.

CUTTING GOTHIC SHAPES FROM MDF

Andy worked with us to cut a range of Gothic motifs from MDF:

■ First sketch your shapes out onto paper from reference material then transfer the shapes to pattern paper.

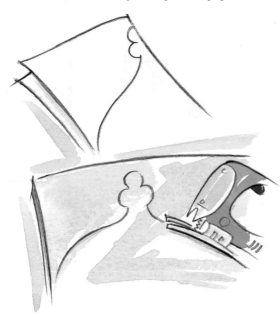

MAKING UP & PAINTING THE DOORS

Andy helped us to create some splendid metal-effect doors:

■ Draw the dimensions of your doors onto paper. Draw half a Gothic arch within these dimensions and draw in the second half to match the first. (Use this technique for the pelmet, bedhead and corona.)

■ Place carbon paper on top of MDF and put the template on top. Trace around the image with a pencil. Cut out the shapes with a jigsaw. For intricate shapes, use a narrow jigsaw blade and

you may need to cut close to the lines first, returning to refine once the bulk of the shape has been cut out.

■ Sand the doors and apply primer (we used one coat of Grey spray primer then Silver spray primer over the top for the arches and doors).

■ When dry (about an hour), use panel adhesive to fix the MDF arches in position. Hold the MDF for a few minutes to 'fix', but it will take an hour or so for the glue to bond completely.

■ Sand the MDF with a power sander fitted with medium-grade sandpaper, then apply a second coat of primer.

■ Next, spray black spray paint over the silver to give a shaded effect to the detailed areas. Add door handles and nail roofing clouts in lines on the doors.

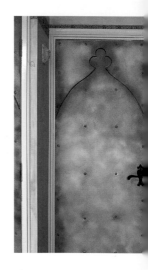

The door arches were cut from MDF. Andy carefully worked round the shaped details with a fine jigsaw blade.

MATERIALS & EQUIPMENT
Scrap paper and pencil
Retractable tape measure
Pattern paper and carbon paper
MDF sheeting (1.3cm/½in thick)
Jigsaw with thin and regular blades
7.5cm (3in) brushes
Spray polyurethane varnish
Rawlplugs and power screwdriver

GOTHIC DOORS
Power sander fitted with medium-grade sandpaper
Spray primers (we used Grey and Silver)
Panel adhesive
Aerosol paint (Silver and Black)
Black door handles

Power drill and hacksaw
Black roofing clouts (nails)
Small hammer

WARDROBE PELMET, CORONA & BEDHEAD
Fixing blocks
Hot melt glue gun
Wooden beads
Metallic paint (we used Gold)
Long wood screws
Piano hinges
Right-angled fixing brackets
Vinyl matt emulsion (we used Basque Brown)
Long-bristled artist's brush
Matt emulsion (we used King's Blue and Carousel Red)
Thick gold pen

MAKING THE PELMET, CORONA & BEDHEAD

Andy helped us to make the wardrobe pelmet, corona and bedhead out of MDF:

■ Construct the pelmet in an 'L' shape to fit on top of the wardrobe and into a corner of the room. Join the MDF with fixing blocks. (Measure the length to determine the longest side, then measure the return for the shortest.)

■ Use three pieces of MDF for the corona: one shaped piece for the front and two side pieces. Measure from the wall to the front of the corona for the depth and measure the front of the corona for the width of the front piece. Glue beads on the crown and paint (we used Gold metallic).

■ Measure the width of the bed to determine the bedhead width, add on 30cm (12in) to each side and divide into four. Two fourths of the measurement equals the centre panel and one fourth remains for each side. The centre panel tapers upwards to meet the corona, while the corona sides are fixed onto the shaped panel using pre-drilled and countersunk screws from the back.

■ Use piano hinges to hold the bedhead sides. The pelmet and corona are fixed to the wall with right-angled fixing brackets screwed through both the wall and MDF. Finally, cut an MDF motif using a template and secure with panel adhesive. Apply beads as for the corona.

PAINTING THE BED & WARDROBE SHAPES

The bed and wardrobe were painted in a vinyl matt emulsion base (we used Basque Brown) and then lined details were added for definition:

■ First draw a light pencil mark around the shapes using your finger as a spacer. Use a long-bristled artist's brush to paint in the lines (we used King's Blue, Carousel Red and thick gold pen). Leave the lining to dry for about an hour. Finally, seal and protect the surface with a layer of spray polyurethane varnish. Leave the varnish to dry for at least an hour.

Use a fine artist's brush to create the lined details on the bed and wardrobe shapes.

PUTTING THE LOOK TOGETHER

Liz found a strong navy blue fabric that complemented the blue of the floor cloth. Black metal curtain poles and a candelabra completed the Gothic effect.

CREATING THE FABRIC TREATMENTS

Curtain poles were fixed above the architrave to prevent daylight from spilling through. To achieve a similar effect:

■ Use single widths of unlined fabric (we used midnight blue), hem the raw edges for each curtain and allow the fabric to crumple at floor level. Sew tabs (we made ours from 23 x 10cm/9 x 4in fabric rectangles) across the curtain tops. (Each tab was hemmed then folded in half across the longest side and sewn to the top of the curtain.) Thread the curtain pole through each loop. Lightweight cotton muslin curtains were threaded onto curtain wires and hung behind the main curtains.

■ The drapes that hung from the wardrobe pelmet were strips of red and blue fabric (each strip was hemmed and stapled at the back of the pelmet).

SPECKLED STONE BEDSIDE TABLES

The original black ash bedside tables were painted to resemble speckled stone:

■ Sand the table with medium-grade sandpaper and apply emulsion (we used Magnolia) using a 7.5cm (3in) brush.

■ Once dry (allow an hour), stipple emulsion (we used White) over the surface using a thick round artist's brush. Leave to dry for one hour.

■ Thin some artist's acrylic colours (we used Yellow Ochre and Raw Umber) with a little water. Using the same brush (while the paint is still wet), stipple the colours over the whole surface.

■ When the speckled finish is dry (in about an hour), protect the table by applying a clear, solid furniture beeswax with a soft cloth and then buff the surface with a duster.

■ Finally, staple a hemmed piece of curtain fabric (we chose blue) around the top edge of the table, gathering the fabric slightly. Glue a strip of fabric trimming over the line of staples using a hot melt glue gun. (It dries in seconds.)

STONE CHEST OF DRAWERS & MATCHING MIRROR

The chest of drawers and mirror frame were painted and embellished with ink-tinted decoupage, enlarged and reduced on a photocopier:

■ Wipe the woodwork down thoroughly with a mild sugar soap solution.

■ Next, spray the surface of the chest of

This bedside table was a cleverly disguised cabinet that had blue fabric stapled onto the top. The staples were covered with a length of matching trimming.

drawers with aerosol paint (we used Silver). Aim to build up a patchy finish.

■ The mirror was treated in the same way but the mirrored area was masked off carefully prior to spraying.

■ Once the aerosol paint is dry, decorate the sides of the chest of drawers with ink-tinted Gothic arches (see page 75). Cut the images out of sheets of paper with sharp scissors and brush PVA adhesive onto the reverse of the copies. Press the photocopies down onto the chest of drawers with your hands. Decorate the sides of the mirror too with longer strips of decoupage.

■ When the PVA adhesive has dried, apply glaze to the decoupage on both the chest of drawers and the mirror as for the walls (see page 75) to give a dusty effect to the entire decoration.

■ Replace old drawer handles on the chest of drawers with knobs. (Ours were hand painted with Princess Blue, then sprayed Silver.) Seal with varnish.

FINISHING TOUCHES

A candlelabra-style light fitting replaced the old centre light fitting. It used attractive, shaped candle bulbs that added to the unique effect of the room. Blood-red wilted roses were placed in the stone-effect urn and Liz tied up bundles of letters and lit red candles to convey the sense of drama. A red bedcover was

quickly made up by hemming a piece of fabric and deep blue fabric was used to cover the cushions. Finally, the shades on the bedside lamps were decorated with some decoupage motifs.

Above: Liz found a wealth of accessories to complete the Gothic look including some atomizers, rich red roses (these were deliberately wilted) and a stone-effect urn. The flame-shaped light bulbs (left) are so effective when used on their own that there is no need for lightshades.

period-look DINING ROOM

Victoria and James' dining room is in the basement of a town house which is identical to that of their friends and neighbours, Mint and Archie. Several aspects of the room pleased Laurence Llewelyn-Bowen and I had the feeling that he was secretly rather pleased with his lot.

A brick-red quarry tiled floor had been laid in both the breakfast room and the adjoining kitchen area. There was also an original black fire surround and wooden shutters were fitted onto two sash windows. These folded back neatly when they were not being used. Tongue-and-groove panelling was fitted onto two of the walls and the fitted cupboards were undoubtedly early Victorian.

Mint explained to Laurence that although James and Victoria had their family roots in the Highlands, she was anxious not to play up the Scottish theme. Recently, Victoria had decorated the toilet in a tartan paint finish and she implied that this was as far as they wanted to go. Archie, however, suggested that Laurence should stencil scottie dogs and bagpipes on the walls.

Laurence felt that he was lucky to be working with such good existing architecture but he was keen to introduce some livelier colours. Mint, however, explained that she wanted to use tasteful, historical hues. Laurence was undeterred by this and persuaded them both that a pot of bright blue and green paint would be just the thing.

Right: The original tongue-and-groove wall cladding needed attention but Mint's original plans were superseded by Laurence's more lively blue and green scheme (left).

GETTING STARTED

A Baronial dining room was the inspiration for the room design. Laurence had uncovered the coat of arms from Victoria's side of the family and was determined to use it in the room.

DESIGNER'S INSPIRATION BOARD

The paint colours that Laurence had chosen for the design scheme were, as far as Mint and Archie were concerned, rather startling. They had suggested that the tongue-and-groove panelling should be completely stripped of paint and the woodwork should be left in its natural state and simply protected with beeswax. However, Laurence had done his research and, in fact, it was never the original intention for the panelling in such a room to be stripped; it was always supposed to be painted. At about the time when these houses were first built the woodwork would have traditionally been painted or stained in a rich, dark colour. In fact, the colours that were used were a more upbeat version of the paints that would have been originally applied and the technique of using two colours together gave a suggestion of age and faded grandeur.

Once Laurence had decided on the colours for the woodwork, other plans fell quickly into place. The walls needed to be lighter in tone so that the scheme was not overwhelming. As red stencilling was to be applied afterwards, a magnolia base colour was felt appropriate. The stencilling technique was unusual in that a red felt-tipped permanent pen was used in preference to conventional paints. A simple cross-hatching method gave a three-dimensional quality that resembled sewing stitches rather than stencilling. Contemporary checkered fabric was chosen as it reflected the colours used in the room and, although not quite tartan, it did have a similar effect whilst not going completely over the top.

The Scottish theme in the room wasn't played up too much. Checks replaced more complicated tartans as these could easily have looked too contrived.

PREPARING THE WALLS, CEILING & WOODWORK

Traditional paint finishes and period details really made the room.

▨ Wipe down the walls and ceiling with warm, soapy water and then apply a base coat of emulsion (we used one-coat Magnolia for this). Use a roller to apply a solid coat of paint, cutting in with a 5cm (2in) brush.

▨ Wipe the painted woodwork clean with a solution of sugar soap. (Wear rubber gloves for this.) This product is specially formulated to remove deposits which can build up on an old, painted surface prior to painting. Use fairly dark paint colours (we used Jade and Pacific Blue) to continue the period look.

CLEANING THE FLOOR TILES

The quarry tiles were cleaned with industrial floor cleaner to give them a new lease of life. When cleaning your own tiles, always get professional advice as to which product you should use and whether any specialist equipment is necessary. Leave the tiles overnight to dry thoroughly and make sure that the room is kept well ventilated.

TILING THE FIREPLACE

Although it would have been great to install a real fire within the fireplace, unfortunately, it was not something that could be done within the tight budget and allocated time. Tiling (see page 153) was the favoured option.

Rich blue tiles are a perfect background for Victoria's collection of copper kitchen utensils. When tiling an area such as a fireplace, measure the space that you need to tile carefully to calculate how many tiles you need and allow a few extra for cuts and breakages.

CHECKLIST

DAY ONE:
- Wash walls, ceiling and woodwork
- Apply emulsion to walls and ceiling
- Clean the floor tiles
- Tile and grout fireplace
- Assemble skirting and fix mirrors to overmantle and shutters
- Fix Georgian-style panelling (available in kit form)
- Apply base coat to woodwork and dresser
- Design, sketch out and cut stencils
- Distress woodwork and dresser
- Apply paint stripper to the mirrors in the shutters and overmantle

DAY TWO
- Apply stencils
- Sew blinds and ties and fix in place
- Make up and fix box pelmets in position
- Upholster chairs
- Assemble overmantle
- Make tabletop and add accessories

PERIOD PAINTWORK

The soft distressed colours used for the wood-work and dresser were an intrinsic part of the whole look. Ordinary solvent-based paints were used to build up layers of colour.

VICTORIAN-STYLE SKIRTINGS

A room of this period would usually have a deep and heavy skirting but these were prohibitively expensive. Andy had a neat solution to the problem, however, using lengths of ordinary MDF:

■ Use a jigsaw to cut two strips of MDF, one slightly less than the required depth of 10cm (4in) and the second piece 7.5cm (3in). Position the smaller strip at the front of the two pieces and then secure both pieces to the wall using rawlplugs and long screws.

■ Panel-pin a strip of decorative picture moulding to the top of the new skirting.

Self-adhesive panels, such as the ones shown here, are available in kit form. The self-adhesive backing tape allows each panel to be effort-lessly positioned, even without the help of Handy Andy!

was used to position the panels between the dado and skirting.

■ To position panels correctly, measure the distance between dado and skirting and then subtract the height of the panel from this. Divide the subsequent measurement into two to give you an even spacing at the top and bottom.

FAKE WALL PANELLING

Period-style panelling was applied to the area below the dado rail. The panels were pre-cut and pre-mitred pieces of self-adhesive mouldings from a DIY store. All that Laurence needed to do was to simply measure the area where the panelling was to be fixed and to stick each part of the moulding in place. (Panel pins are not required for this.) The dining room already had a wooden dado rail in place and, with a spirit level, this

SCOTTISH-STYLE STENCILS

To achieve cross-hatched stencils, use a permanent red marker pen. First, use a scalpel to cut your own stencil from manilla card and then position each motif randomly on the wall with repositionable spray adhesive. Cross-hatch parts of the motif to create a shadow effect.

MATERIALS & EQUIPMENT

DISTRESSED PAINT FINISH

Medium-grade sandpaper

White wood primer

7.5cm (3in) and 2.5cm (1in) brushes

Non-drip gloss (we used Jade and Pacific Blue)

Wax candle

Soft cloths

White spirit

CREATING A DISTRESSED PAINT FINISH

The blue and green distressed effect was used on the dresser and woodwork for an eighteenth-century feel.

■ Sand and, if necessary, prime the wood with white wood primer using a 7.5cm (3in) brush and a 2.5cm (1in) brush for the tongue-and-groove recesses. Leave the primer to dry for about two hours. Once dry, apply a coat of the first colour (we used Jade) using the same-sized brush as before and allow two hours for the paint to dry.

■ Rub a warmed candle over the dry paint surface paying particular attention to the corners and those areas that would normally receive the most wear and tear. Finally, apply the second colour (Pacific Blue) in the same way as before and leave for two hours to dry.

■ Dampen a cloth with white spirit and rub this over the painted surface. The

underlying wax prevents the top layer of paint from adhering to the first layer of colour and the cloth will start to remove the colour quite quickly. To finish, wipe the surface with a clean cloth.

Although Mint had tried to prevent the dresser from being painted, in the end everyone loved the distressed effect. Pretty china became more prominent against the painted background.

PUTTING THE LOOK TOGETHER

China, wicker baskets, copper kitchenware and even a Scottish-style sconce were some of the details that really made the room. Checkered fabric matched the room colours perfectly.

CHECKED BLINDS & DECORATIVE TIES

Minimal sewing skills are required for this effective window treatment.

■ Cut a rectangle of fabric to the same size as the window, hem and secure it onto a 5 x 2.5cm (2 x 1in) timber batten with Velcro fastening tape.

A staple gun was used to quickly re-cover the seat backs of these elegant dining chairs.

■ Screw the batten onto the window frame and then fit box pelmets over the top of the blind to conceal any unsightly fixings (see page 152). These are constructed with MDF and an attractive strip of moulding is applied to the top of the pelmets to further emphasize the character of the room. It is glued into place with wood glue and panel-pinned every 25cm (10in) or so.

■ The fabric is held bunched, just below the pelmet, using two ties made from the same fabric. Cut a strip of fabric to the same length as the window drop. Fold the edges to the inside along the length of fabric on both sides, then fold them in half and stitch to close.

■ Finally, staple two ties (use the same fabric) at the front (and two at the back) of the blind about 15cm (6in) in from the sides of the window frames.

SIMPLE UPHOLSTERED CHAIRS

The dining chairs were reupholstered in the same checked fabric as the blinds:

▪ Position a square of fabric over the seat of a chair and staple along the front, turning the excess fabric underneath. Use the same technique for the

chair back, leaving both sides free for mitring afterwards. Finally, turn the sides under in the same way and fold each corner under and staple into place.

AGEING THE MIRRORS

The insides of the shutter panels were glazed with antiqued mirror. (A glazier will cut mirrors to your requirements.) In the evening soft candlelight would be reflected back in the mirrors. To do this:

▪ Use a small brush to apply paint stripper to the coated mirror back.

▪ Remove the stripper with a cloth and dispose of the residue carefully (refer to the manufacturer's recommendations).

▪ Wash the mirrors with water and a cloth and glue to the shutters with a strong adhesive. (This holds in minutes.)

▪ A similar piece of mirror was fixed onto a shaped piece of MDF that was to

be the overmantle. To create the same look, shape the top of the mirror frame using a jigsaw (see pages 148–9). Secure with adhesive, then use strips of moulding to decorate the plain sides of the frame using the same adhesive. Distress as for the woodwork.

FINISHING TOUCHES

Finally, Andy created a tabletop from reclaimed floorboards. These were battened together and antiquing wax was applied with a soft cloth. Victoria's ceramic pieces decorated the fireplace together with pots of heather, frosted fruit was placed on the tabletop and the candles were rekindled. The combination of period panelling and contemporary stencilling was a complete success.

A glazier drilled a hole in the mirror (above) to hold the sconce, and candles were placed in front of the shutter mirrors (below).

multi-purpose BEDROOM

Mint and Archie have an elegant townhouse that they moved into just over a year ago. Their children's bedroom needed reorganizing and we needed to do something about the floral wallpaper; also there was limited storage space. James and Victoria, the neighbours who worked with me, were keen to give the children some bunk beds and this would certainly free up a lot of space. They also wanted to introduce an element of Shaker style with a set of pegs or even a rail. Two clear ideas began to formulate: first, an American folk art style with tongue-and-groove panelling, peg rails and motifs and secondly, a bright, jazzy look using bold colours and strong patterns. The Shaker idea was the most appealing but it seemed too sophisticated for two lively young children. We decided to combine the themes with bold colours and painted walls but we also wanted to add a gingham pattern and to make a feature of some long peg rails.

I opted for Roman blinds at the window with unlined fabric panels at the sides and we decided to paint directly onto the hardboard floor.

As the children were both young, I wanted to give their bedroom a theme and my imagination was sparked off by a kind of 'down at the bottom of the garden' idea. I used garden images and motifs for an individual look.

Fortunately, the busy floral wallpaper (right) was not a vinyl paper which meant that emulsion paint could be applied directly over the walls to create the lively gingham checkered pattern (left).

GETTING STARTED

One of my favourite plants, euphorbia, was growing in the garden at the time that I chose the main colour for the room and this perhaps swayed my choice. It was not quite an acid green but more of a green ochre.

DESIGNER'S INSPIRATION BOARD

If you look at a piece of gingham fabric carefully you will notice the way in which the coloured blocks build up into their own characteristic style of pattern. Columns of alternate dark, then medium tones of a colour lie side by side with columns of medium and light tones. This formula was the basis for the paint effect that was used on the walls of the children's room.

We wanted to include several Shaker-style references and a charming postcard that depicted a wonderful old picket fence was adapted into an idea. A New England-style picket fence would be a good way of disguising clutter: it would be quick to knock up and, with the sharp edges rounded off, nice and safe for use in a children's room. Armed with this plan for a clever way to hide and store the children's toys and clothes, together with ideas for a smart peg rail running across one of the walls, I felt that the request for Shaker style had been addressed rather neatly. I also had plans to decorate the bed posts with intricate cockerel and daisy motifs.

PAINTED FLOOR FINISH

Andy stapled down a new hardboard floor (see page 153) and then the primed floor was given two coats of emulsion (we used Beckett Blue):

Children's rooms are a delight to design. I looked at jazzy-coloured checks and ginghams and drew my inspiration for the wall finish from these.

CHECKLIST

DAY ONE:
- Remove carpet and old curtains
- Staple down primed hardboard for floor
- Apply base coat and varnish to floor
- Paint walls and woodwork
- Mark up squares on wall
- Paint in gingham effect and paint ceiling
- Make and install peg rail

DAY TWO:
- Build and paint picket fences
- Apply paint and decoupage to storage chest
- Stamp the fabric for the blind
- Make up blinds, banners and drawstring bags
- Fix up and decorate lighting collar
- Hang the Tarzan rope
- Paint chest of drawers
- Paint bed parts and assemble bed
- Make flower and cockerel posts for bed

■ Use 10cm (4in) brushes to cover the floor area quickly with paint. Allow an hour between coats.

■ When the second coat is dry (after an hour) apply two layers of acrylic varnish. Again, allow at least an hour between coats.

GINGHAM-LOOK WALLS

A chequered green painted pattern was used to liven up the nursery walls. To recreate the look:

■ Apply a base colour of paint (we used Lady Mantle matt vinyl) to cover the wallpaper and paint the ceiling in the same colour using a wide 10cm (4in) brush. (The colour we chose was a medium tone used in a piece of gingham fabric.)

■ After one hour, apply a top coat to both the walls and ceiling to completely cover the surface using the same brush.

■ Paint the woodwork at this stage using a satinwood paint (we used Lady Mantle) and a 5cm (2in) brush. Allow the colour to dry (about two hours).

■ Measure each wall up carefully and divide into 30cm (12in) squares. Draw horizontal lines across the walls using a spirit level and drop a chalked plumb line at intervals of 30cm (12in). Secure the chalked line at ceiling height then

allow the plumb to settle and hold it tight against the wall. To transfer the chalk, ping the taut line.

■ Grid up the whole room then start to paint in the gingham effect using the lighter colour (we used Chinois) and the darker colour (Sundew). Outline each square first with a 2.5cm (1in) brush and then fill in with a 5cm (2in) brush.

Use a piece of gingham fabric to plan out your colour scheme for the walls. Follow the combination of light, medium and dark colours for an authentic effect.

PICKET GATE DOORS

Storage is always a priority in a child's environment and in this small room we needed to address the needs of two young children.

A large chest of drawers, just outside the room, could cope with most items of clothing. Two shallow alcoves on either side of the chimney breasts were ideal storage areas and the idea of two picket gates seemed a great alternative to the more familiar cupboard doors. They would really help to enforce the colourful garden theme. Andy's carpentry skills were put to good use for this project:

MATERIALS & EQUIPMENT

7 timber lengths, 8 x 13cm (3 x 5in)
Paper and pencil
Jigsaw
Medium-grade sandpaper
2 timber lengths, 6 x 2.5cm (2 x 1in)
Spirit level
Drill fitted with a wood drill bit
No. 4 screws

Batten cut from 5 x 2.5cm (2 x 1in) finished timber
Ready-mixed filler
10cm (4in) brushes
Acrylic primer
Vinyl matt emulsion (we used Achievement)
Clear acrylic varnish
Latches and hinges

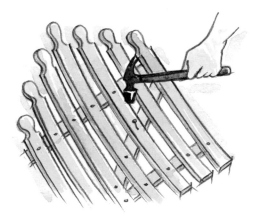

■ Cut seven lengths of timber 8 x 13cm (3 x 5in). The central post is placed at the highest point and the other lengths should graduate downwards, symmetrically at both sides. Shape the top of the lengths with a paper template, first mark the outlines in pencil, then cut round with a jigsaw and sand the edges.

■ Cut two pieces of 6 x 2.5cm (2 x 1in) timber for the horizontal supports at the back of the gate. The measurement should equal the alcove width, less about 1cm (⅓in) for the hinges. Lay the vertical posts evenly across the two horizontals. Drill, countersink and screw together. Turn the fence over and cut a

crossways batten to fit between the supports. Secure with screws from the front.

■ Fill the holes with filler, prime and then apply a base coat. When dry (allow about an hour), protect with a coat of acrylic varnish and leave to dry according to the manufacturer's recommendations. Fix latches and hinges onto mounting blocks, then secure to fences.

SHAKER PEG RAILS

Andy fitted rails of pegs that were perfect for hanging drawstring bags and, in time, the children would be able to hang clothes, toys or whatever they wished from them. The small nesting box drawer

The picket gate doors, painted in the same colour as the floor (Achievement), fenced off useful storage areas in the children's bedroom. Continuing the storage theme, little drawstring bags were made from assorted scraps of fabric. I inserted zigzag edging in a contrasting fabric along the lower hem of some of the bags to vary the look.

was a special secret hiding place that the children would love.

■ Drill 5 x 5cm (2 x 2in) timber lengths to hold 25mm (1in) dowelling. Tap the dowelling into the holes (apply glue for added strength) with a mallet. Plane off the edges and paint (we used Chinois).

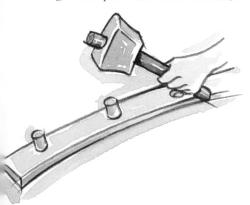

DECOUPAGED CHEST
Dual-purpose items of furniture are always useful where space is limited and here the storage chest also serves as a seat. It was the most expensive item that we purchased for the room but it was worth it.

■ We sanded, primed and painted the chest with emulsion (Chinois). Once the paint was dry (allow an hour for each coat), decoupage motifs (see page 36) were applied randomly.

PUTTING THE LOOK TOGETHER

It was the garden references (photographs of allotments and illustrations from children's books) that really brought the whole design scheme together.

Continuing the garden theme, a range of projects were designed for the room.

PRINTING THE ROMAN BLIND

The blind fabric was made to look fabulous with a little printed beetroot motif. (Use fabric paint for this.)

■ To make up a printing block, copy your chosen motif onto 3mm (⅛in) foam rubber using a paper pattern and cut out with a scalpel. (We used a patterned plate as a reference for the motif.) Fix the foam onto a small offcut of timber with contact adhesive (follow the manufacturer's instructions) to make a small printing block.

If you use a checked fabric, such as this one, to print out your design then it is easy to position your printing block as no measuring out is necessary.

MAKING THE BLIND

■ Measure the window and cut two pieces of cloth allowing 5cm (2in) extra all round for a seam allowance.

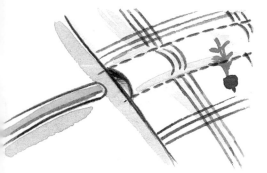

■ Sew the edges together leaving a small turning gap. Turn the fabric right side out and sew long pockets to hold each length of dowelling. Each rod pocket is sewn horizontally across the blind and the rods, cut to the width of the blind, are inserted. Use eyelets and cord to raise and lower the blind.

DECORATIVE BANNERS

Two plain fabric banners (the width of a piece of fabric) were hemmed and slot-headed on a black pole. Boldly-checked fabric echoed the colours used elsewhere in the room.

■ To make an attractive finish, apply fringed edging along three sides of each banner. Fray lengths of woven fabric and machine-stitch onto the banners.

LIGHTING COLLAR

The lighting collar was cut from MDF and painted in emulsion (we used Chinois). This was secured around a paper shade in the centre of the ceiling.

■ Take a piece of string and secure to the MDF with a drawing pin. Tie a pencil at the other end to make a compass. Draw two circles, one 20cm (8in) inside the other. Cut out, then attach the collar to the ceiling with timber fixing blocks and long screws that fix into the joists.

FINISHING TOUCHES

Continuing the lively gingham theme throughout the room, some drawstring fabric bags were made up. The chest of drawers was prepared and painted with two coats of matt emulsion (we used Chinois) and varnished. Wooden bunk beds (available in kit form) were painted (we used Achievement) and assembled once the paint was dry, then MDF flower and cockerel motifs on posts were added.

Both parents and children were highly delighted with the result which demonstrates the amazing effects that can be achieved with bold use of colour.

Fake vegetables, insects and fun accessories (above) were strung from cotton threads tied to small hooks that were fixed to the ceiling collar. A knotted tarzan rope (below) makes it quite simple for the occupant of the top bunk bed to descend to the floor!

country BEDROOM

The three-storey town house, in which Ann and Ron live, is elegant and modern but their main problem was that everything was either mismatched or just completely out of place. Their bedroom was a typical example of this problem: old louvre-doored wardrobes and dark green painted walls were teamed with an awkward staircase leading to the attic. However, the room was spacious and full of natural light.

Graham Wynne, the designer working on the room, liked the proportions and had already started to formulate ideas for a French country-style design. He had spotted a few elegant pieces of furniture in the house that could be used more effectively in the bedroom and was keen to make the most of them. Traci and Tony, who worked with Graham, were looking forward to transforming the room and were more than happy to contribute ideas.

Very soon the dark green paint on the walls was on its way out and Graham began to plot the fate of the old-fashioned wardrobes. He wanted to update their look by getting rid of the doors and reworking some new ones. Graham was more than a little nervous when he suggested that the staircase to the loft above should be smashed down but he needn't have worried. Traci and Tony soon relegated it to the skip and then the work really started.

Graham completely altered the look of the original room in Chester (right). Once the staircase was removed, it allowed him greater freedom to work with the space (left).

GETTING STARTED

A blue and white colour scheme was the start of the elegant, yet relaxed look for the French country bedroom.

DESIGNER'S INSPIRATION BOARD

Ann and Ron had built up their collection of antique pine furniture over the years so there was an excess. This meant that Graham and Traci had plenty to choose from when they were selecting suitable pieces for the bedroom.

Blue and white became the strongest accent colours. Ready-made curtains in bold blue stripes, blue throws and cushions added a splash of colour. The wardrobes too were given a coat of French blue paint that was aged effectively using tinted furniture wax.

DECONSTRUCTING THE STAIRCASE

The main task for Andy was to take apart the staircase that led up to the attic and to install a loft ladder (see page 153). At least one third of the bedroom area had been lost to the staircase and, as the loft was only used as a storage space, a modern lightweight ladder was needed.

PAINTING THE WALLS, CEILING & WOODWORK

The walls and ceiling were covered with Brilliant White emulsion (we used one-coat paint that dries in an hour) and added a scumble glaze:

■ Use a roller to apply the emulsion and cut in with a 5cm (2in) brush.

■ Next, use a ready-mixed tinted scumble glaze (we used Stonewash White). Apply with a (7.5cm/3in) brush using a scrubbing technique. While the paint is still damp, soften brush strokes with a dry cloth. Leave to dry for one hour.

A classic combination of crisp whites and blues was put together for the room. Traditional stripes and gingham fabrics set the tone for the inspiration board.

CHECKLIST

DAY ONE:
- Source pieces of furniture and ceramics
- Remove staircase and replace with loft ladder
- Base coat walls and ceiling and apply scumble glaze to the walls
- Paint skirting and doors with white eggshell paint
- Paint floor
- Apply floor glaze and use woodgrainer
- Paint in floorboards with marker pen
- Create headboard
- Remove wardrobe doors, sand and base coat body of wardrobe
- Cut out the wardrobe panels
- Spray chicken wire black and secure
- Staple gingham behind wire
- Replace wardrobe handles

DAY TWO:
- Fix ruched gingham over door
- Make and hang drape over bed
- Sew muslin drapes
- Put up curtain rails and hang drapes
- Make ottoman
- Apply graining to picture frames
- Add panels to doors

The skirting boards and doors were painted white with an oil-based eggshell paint. (Use a 7.5cm/3in brush and allow at least two hours before recoating.)

MOCK-GRAINED FLOORS & 'HEADBOARD'

The floor and mock headboard were painted in a natural linen colour:

Apply flexible filler to the gaps between flooring with a flexible knife. Once dry (about an hour), sand and remove dust. Apply a base coat of paint (we used Mink satinwood). Leave for two hours.

Next, apply a layer of glaze with a 7.5cm (3in) brush. (We used one part white emulsion and one part Stonewash scumble glaze mixed with one part clear scumble glaze.)

Gently rock a woodgraining rocker over the still-wet glazed boards. Work in sections and wipe away build-up on the rocker with a cotton rag. When dry, paint in the floorboard lines with a black marker pen and leave overnight.

Paint the headboard area as above, then mitre and screw wooden moulding into the wall around the painted 'head-board' area to complete the illusion. The moulding is then painted (we used Mink satinwood) and grained to match.

A classic blue and white scheme (left) was Graham's starting point for the design. Mock-grained floorboards (right) are perfect for those who love the effect of wooden flooring but can't afford the real thing.

FRENCH FARMHOUSE WARDROBE

Graham changed the wardrobes quite significantly. The new doors had four panels which were jigsawed out and then replaced with painted chicken wire and gingham fabric.

Replacement doors were integral for the look of this new wardrobe. They can be purchased from many DIY stores for a very reasonable price. Check that the doors will fit your own wardrobe. Unfinished pine is preferable to any varnished or lacquered finish as it will accept a paint treatment without any prior preparation. To create your own distressed wardrobe:

■ Use wooden cornicing (cut to match the front and sides of the wardrobe) to build up a detailed edge at the top of the wardrobe. Mitre the corners. Mark out and cut the moulding with a tenon saw and use long wood screws and wood glue to fix it in place. Drill and countersink pilot holes for screws. Fill the holes in, then paint (see opposite).

■ Fix a skirting board measuring the width of your wardrobe base at the bottom of the wardrobe. Mitre the edges and countersink each screw.

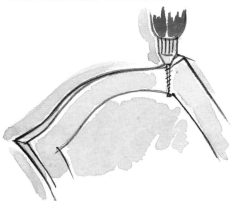

■ To remove the centre panels from each door, place them flat on a work bench. Make a pilot hole with a drill bit

MATERIALS & EQUIPMENT

Reclaimed cornice (approximately 10cm/4in deep)
Mitre block
Pencil
Tenon saw
Long wood screws
Wood glue (for extra security on mitred sections)
Drill fitted with a wood drill bit
Filler and filler knife
Skirting board (to match existing boards or 20cm/8in deep)
Jigsaw
Medium-grade sandpaper
Chicken wire (we used 1.8m/6ft)
Tin snips or pliers
Staple gun
Small hammer
Gingham or your chosen fabric (about 2m/7ft)
Dressmaker's scissors
Sewing machine
Matching thread
Replacement handles

large enough to allow the saw blade to pass through. Work round the panel slowly with the jigsaw. Sand the rough edges with medium-grade sandpaper.

■ Turn the door over to work on the inside. Cut the chicken-wire to size using tin snips or pliers. Cut the wire approximately 2.5cm (1in) wider all round than the panel itself.

■ Staple the wire across the length of one of the shortest sides. Hold it taut and staple across the opposite side. Staple at the centre of both of the longest sides of wire, then work towards the corners keeping it taut as you progress. Tap in any staples that may be raised above the frame using a hammer and turn sharp edges inwards with your fingers.

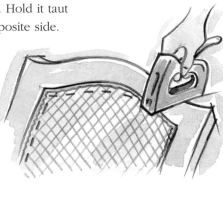

Right: If you thought that gingham fabrics could never look smart and sophisticated, then think again. Here the combination of blue and white against the distressed paintwork works brilliantly.

■ The fabric panels should be cut to size allowing an extra 5cm (2in) all round. Stitch a narrow hem on all four sides using a sewing machine and matching thread, then staple the fabric over the chicken wire at the back of each door panel. Finally, replace the wardrobe handles with new ones.

PAINTING THE WARDROBE

Once the wardrobe was restructured by Andy, the surface was distressed:

■ First lightly sand and apply a coat of white acrylic primer using a 7.5cm (3in) brush. Allow an hour for drying.

■ Next, apply a coat of buff-coloured

RUCHED FABRIC WARDROBE PANELS
You may prefer to use gathered fabric for the panels. Cut the fabric one and a half times the required width, adding 5cm (2in) for turnings. Hem as for flat panels and fold the top edges under again by another 2.5cm (1in) to form a channel for net curtain wires and secure these at the back of the doors with curtain hooks.

emulsion and wait for it to dry. Then using the same brush, brush a coat of emulsion (we used Regal Blue) over the surface. Leave the paint to dry for at least an hour.

■ Finally, apply antiquing wax carefully over the whole of the dry paint surface using a pad of wire wool. Some of the top coat of paint will be rubbed away, revealing the buff colour underneath. This gives the illusion of aged paint with the wood showing through and adds character to the wardrobe.

PUTTING THE LOOK TOGETHER

The blue and white colour scheme was continued at the windows, on the bed and even on the floor to bring the design together.

Basic, natural country cottons were used in the bedroom. Gingham was used for most of the soft furnishings – the wardrobe panels and ottoman in particular made good use of this crisp, inexpensive cloth. Striped ticking fabric hung at the window. This was, in fact, a pair of ready-made curtains with a slot heading. The combination of small checks and bold stripes in the room was a perfect balance. Often some of the most successful interiors have clever combinations of pattern and texture.

BED CANOPY

A ready-made voile curtain was tied onto a semi-circular frame (available from some DIY stores). To make your own:

▧ Measure the drop with a piece of string. Add a gentle loop and then another 15cm (6in) for a generous hem to bunch onto the floor. Measure the string and cut your fabric accordingly.

▧ Cut white ribbon ties (about 20cm/8in long) from cotton dressmaker's tape and sew these onto the top of the voile turning the raw edges under as you sew. Tie the ribbons onto the frame.

▧ To make the tiebacks, cut strips (about 30cm/12in long) from ticking and hem. Staple onto the headboard.

WINDOW DRAPES

Muslin allowed light into the room whilst maintaining privacy. These drapes were made up from hemmed squares that were gathered at the top and threaded through curtain wires.

GINGHAM-COVERED OTTOMAN

Gingham fabric was cut to the same size as the front, sides and top of the ottoman with an allowance of an extra 5cm (2in) all round for turning. The ottoman was a regular shape, with a plain (padded) lid. The old trimming was ripped away and covered directly over the old fabric. To cover your own ottoman, follow the instructions below:

▧ With a staple gun, carefully cover the front of the box with fabric first and then the back and finally, staple on the side pieces keeping all visible staples to a minimum.

The mock headboard and voile canopy over the half-tester bed (above) add an almost regal touch.

Mounting card (right) was given the same graining effect as the floor. Once dry, it was then positioned around the central image and the picture frame was painted to match.

Graham and Andy used parts of the old staircase (left) to make some new shelving. The thick brackets were, in fact, created from two stair treads that were then glued together.

A ruched gingham panel (below) was fixed onto curtain wires above the door to cover a plain glazed area.

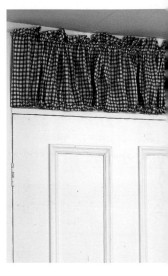

▪ Finally, fold all the raw edges to the inside of the box and repeat for the lid. Leave the inside of the box plain, but cut the fabric close to the line of staples.

FINISHING TOUCHES

In the last hour or two, plain doors were made more interesting by panel-pinning four simple rectangles of wooden moulding to the insets using a nail punch and panel pins. The panel pins were punched below the surface of the wood. These areas were filled and the doors were then given a coat of the same oil-based eggshell paint that was used to paint the skirtings.

Finally, some blue checkered cushions were run up on a sewing machine from remnants of fabric and all the pine furniture was arranged in the room, along with rugs, pictures, lamps and vases of fresh flowers. The finished effect was a resounding success.

nautical ATTIC ROOM

Tony and Traci had an awkward room at the top of their home that was giving them endless decorating problems. Traci was concerned about the children climbing over the banisters as the room was open to the stairs on one side which also meant no privacy at all and so they were keen to make it into a family room.

As well as being a family/playroom space, the room had to incorporate other functions. It needed to be a guest bedroom and also a study area. The biggest problem was that there was simply no order to anything. When Liz Wagstaff, the designer working on this room, took the attic room on board, Traci and Tony were delighted to hand all these problems over to her.

With the space being used for so many functions, Liz had to prioritize the work. Tony required a desk area and room to store papers and files. The room was less frequently used as a spare room – a sofa bed or futon would be the best solution and it could also provide a seating area. For a family room, there needed to be more storage space, easy-to-clean surfaces and an area for relaxing. Traci's parents, Ann and Ron, were enthusiastic and confident about working on the room. They wanted to make everything shipshape for their family and that was just the look that Liz was about to give them.

Right: This room was difficult to organize as it needed to serve several purposes. However, it was a problem that Liz was happy to resolve with some stylish solutions (left).

GETTING STARTED

The nautical theme provided Liz with a perfect design scheme for the room. It would be something that both children and parents could live with, without being too contrived or childish.

DESIGNER'S INSPIRATION BOARD

Liz's research provided her with picture references for boatyards, lighthouses and ship's cabins. She captured the flavour of each of these brilliantly within this small attic room to make it appear like life on the ocean waves with portholes and blinds that resembled rigging. Some great accessories helped the scheme along – seaside buckets painted with hot pink enamel varnish, fishing floats and even a lifesaving ring complete with knotted string. These were all made or acquired inexpensively from junk stores, salvage yards and ship chandler's merchants.

CHOOSING A COLOUR SCHEME

Colour was a primary consideration: it was undoubtedly the most important aspect of the room once the overall design had been devised. This turned out to be the most controversial aspect too, once we discovered that Traci harboured more than a passing grudge towards anything green. Once Liz had chosen the aquamarine colour for the walls, she needed to select a shade from the opposite end of the spectrum to balance its vibrancy. This is an effective trick and it can be adapted to almost every interior. A splash of red against green is a great way of making colours work together. Designers will often use this theory of colour balancing. With this in mind, frames, wickerwork and lamp bases were colour washed in red and on the finer, tongue-and-groove walls a green colour wash was brushed over a white base to add depth and texture.

The aquamarine colour that Liz used conjures up images of the sea, boatyards and fishing boats. Oranges and reds helped to balance the green.

PAINTING THE WALLS & CEILING

The first job was painting and so the carpet was dust-sheeted and taped down at the edges. Preparation for painting is always a dull task however, in order for any painted surface to stand the test of time it must have a good foundation. For Liz, Ann and Ron, this meant lots of sanding as two of the walls were covered from floor to ceiling in tongue-and-groove cladding, followed by a thorough washing-down using sugar soap.

CREATING YOUR OWN COLOURS

The wall cladding was primed and then one coat of white emulsion was applied with a 7.5cm (3in) brush. (Both coats need at least an hour to dry.) The aquamarine colour was mixed up:

■ Squeeze approximately half a tube of colour into a 2.5 litre (½ gallon) paint kettle and thin this with tap water until the colour becomes liquid.

■ Mix approximately half a litre (¹⁄₁₀ gallon) of acrylic scumble glaze into the paint, stirring all the time. Test on scrap paper first and adjust accordingly.

■ Pick up a small amount of paint on a dry brush and reload as appropriate. Use a light brushing technique to give a dragged effect over the wall cladding.

■ Paint the ceiling and the other walls in a matching solid base colour (we used Folklore matt emulsion). Allow about 1½ hours for the glaze to dry.

PORTHOLE CUPBOARD DOORS

Andy replaced the airing cupboard doors with new MDF ones:

■ Drill random 2.5cm (1in) holes right through the doors for ventilation.

■ Apply a base white emulsion and one hour later, brush furniture wax over the whole surface with a 1.3cm (½in) brush.

CHECKLIST

DAY ONE:
- Wash, sand and prime the timber
- Paint walls and ceiling
- Base coat the timber
- Glaze walls
- Cut cupboard doors
- Stencil the floorcloth
- Re-cover worktop
- Colour wash accessories
- Enamel tinware

DAY TWO:
- Paint doors
- Make up blinds
- Hang blinds
- Varnish floor cloth
- Frame pictures and other objects
- Make up tea towel cushions
- Make clock and put up shelves
- Stain futon, work trestles and wooden containers

■ Brush a coat of green paint (we used Folklore) over the top using a 7.5cm (3in) brush. Once dry, gently sand the door to age it.

■ Fix a round mirror to the top of the door with strong glue. Leave to dry according to the package directions.

These porthole doors look extremely elegant and the drilled holes are dual-purpose as they prevent the doors from warping as well as being decorative.

CREATING THE CANVAS EFFECT

Inexpensive calico was used for the window coverings and over shelves for hidden storage. Using brass eyelets, the blinds were strung with cord to look like sails.

UNLINED SAIL BLINDS

These cotton duck blinds are sewn onto a curtain pole and left unlined so that the natural light can filter through. Each blind should be tied onto a pole fixed slightly above the window frame.

■ Measure the width and drop of the window area that you are covering and then add 5cm (2in) all round. Fold the seam allowance to the back of the blind with a double hem. Press with a hot iron and fold each corner neatly. Sew all four sides using a long running stitch on the sewing machine.

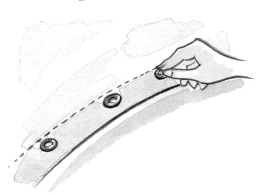

■ Fix the eyelets at regular intervals around the sides and top of the blind. (One eyelet every 20cm/5in should be sufficent.) Most eyelet kits are supplied with a fixing kit. Measure the two longer sides and the one shorter side of the blind for the amount of cord that you will need and add a generous 30cm (12in) to allow for raising and lowering.
■ Take one end of nylon cord and use this to thread up one side of the blind between the eyelets as if you were

MATERIALS & EQUIPMENT

Retractable tape measure
Tailor's chalk
Fabric of your choice
  (we used calico)
Dressmaker's scissors
Sewing machine

Natural cotton polyester thread
Eyelet kit
Nylon cord (about 10–12m/32–39ft
  for an average blind)
Curtain poles, as required
Bulldog clips (allow 2 for each blind)

sewing a running stitch. 'Overstitch' the cord at the top of the blind to 'sew' it onto a curtain pole. (See page 152 for advice on curtain poles.) Continue to sew right down the other side. Pull the cord ends so that each side is level and push the fabric upwards to the required height. Secure with bulldog clips.

MAKING THE FLOORCLOTH

The floorcloth was made from heavy-weight duck canvas which was first stencilled and then varnished:
■ Cut the cloth to fit the floor area. Add an extra 5cm (2in) all round for seam allowance. Fold the allowance to the back of the floorcloth and press with a hot iron. Brush a line of PVA adhesive along the fold line and press flat.

■ Measure the cloth and mark out the positions of 20 signal flags across the width of the fabric.

■ Place stencilling card on a flat cutting surface and mark out your flag design in pencil. Cut out with a craft knife.

■ Lay the stencil to correspond with the positions on the mat then stencil through the card with a stencil brush and fabric paint. Use repositioning spray on the back of the stencil to keep a good contact between fabric and card.

■ Remove the card and allow each flag to dry. (Usually, the paint will be touch-dry in about 10–15 minutes.) Mark around the outlines with a waterproof marker and a ruler, then seal and protect the cloth with acrylic varnish. Leave to dry for an hour, then press on the reverse side. Leave overnight and seal with a layer of acrylic varnish using a 7.5cm (3in) brush. The varnish dries in about 1½–2 hours.

NAUTICAL PICTURES

To continue the seafaring theme, Liz framed some interesting colour photocopies. She used signal flag motifs in addition to several picture postcards.

TEA TOWEL CUSHION COVERS

Liz used tea towels to make her sofa cushions. Follow her simple instructions:

■ Fold each towel in half, with right sides together, and use a matching thread to stitch, leaving a turning gap of approximately 15cm (6in).

■ Turn through, place a cushion pad inside and sew the gap closed.

Lots of cushions were piled up invitingly on the futon sofa bed. A green cotton throw protected the folded mattress and also served as a bedcover whenever it was needed.

PUTTING THE LOOK TOGETHER

Liz's eye for those special finishing touches really brought the whole look together. Items such as the lifesaving ring, toy lighthouse and boat gave the whole room a cabin flavour.

Why not check out your local chandlers or frame your own pieces of flotsam and jetsam from the beach? Shells and pebbles will need a frame with a recessed area underneath the glass. Wooden frames may be stained with coloured wood stain as here (allow an hour for drying) or use a dilute emulsion paint (equal parts paint and water) which dries in about 30 minutes. Sand and paint or varnish frames before repainting.

LIFESAVING RING CLOCK

To make the 'lifesaving ring' clock:

■ Cut a circle out of MDF, then cut a hole in the centre of this to the size of your clock using a jigsaw. Round off the outer edges with a sander. Put your clock in the centre and glue a panel of MDF over the back to hold in place.

■ Fix 8 hooks around the outside of the ring and thread thick sisal rope through these. Paint the rope with white emulsion.

■ Finally, paint the ring in red and white emulstion and, when dry, stencil your name or message on the ring.

SAFE SHELVING

Andy fitted built-in shelf units on the banisters around the stairwell not only to stack the children's toy boxes but also as a safety precaution to prevent the children from climbing over the banisters.

■ Measure the span needed for the double-shelving system and cut the shelving accordingly. (Andy used white conti boards.) The shelves are supported at either end with vertical timber supports screwed into the banisters. For extra strength, Andy also used shelf supports at the centre of each shelf, once again fixing these onto the banisters.

■ The top shelf is fixed directly underneath the stair rail. Drill wood screws to the hand rail from underneath the top shelf, then fix on the shelf supports.

Plastic stacking boxes (left) stored most of the children's toys and books. The coloured plastic meant that it was easy to recognize the contents but it also blended in with the whole scheme.

Above right: When set against the aquamarine colour that was predominantly used throughout the room, nautical accessories made the family room an enjoyable place in which to work and play.

Make sure that each hole has been carefully countersunk first so that it can be later drilled and then painted (we used white emulsion).

FINISHING TOUCHES

The clever use of green paints, stains and glazes, together with flashes of red and hot pink, was a winning combination in this room. Wood stain (Green) was used to finish off the untreated wood on the futon base, chair frame, worktop frame, small shelving units and the storage containers. Stain (Deep Pink) was used on the storage boxes and frames too for contrast and enamel paints brightened up the collection of tinware.

Other accessories such as the wall light were all basic items that, once combined with such vibrancy in a room, suddenly become very covetable. This room has much to do with getting up the courage to put junk store finds together with DIY store bargains and then combining the two with colour and style. Traci and Tony were overwhelmed by their new room – and the green? When it looks as good as this, who could fail to be impressed?

These purchased wall lights gave the room a much softer effect during the evening.

victorian FORMAL ROOM

The main problem for designer Graham Wynne was to decide how to decorate a room that was already quite beautiful. Rav and Michelle appreciated the problem but felt that the style of room really wasn't to their liking. They had purchased the early Victorian house several years ago from an interior designer and had inherited someone else's taste along with it.

Sue and Nigel, their friends and neighbours, wanted to change the overall feel, as they felt that the room was not at all relaxing. However, they loved some of the formal elements – the elegant bay window and marble fireplace – but nothing else seemed to fit. A second reception room, which lay across the hall, had a cosier feeling. Graham decided to switch the furniture in these rooms so that they would serve two definite roles: one for elegant entertaining while the other could become a family room.

There were enough deep red accessories around the house to convince Graham and the neighbours that Rav and Michelle would be happy with a similar colour scheme. The marble fireplace had rich, red tones and a winged armchair was upholstered in this colour. To provide balance, Graham used tones of ivory, cream and calico to ensure that the room would always be bright and welcoming during the day, but rich and sophisticated in the evening.

Left: Graham wanted to paint a darker colour from the picture rails to the skirtings in this room and so he painted the ceiling in a lighter colour to lift the whole effect. It was quite the opposite of the original scheme (right).

GETTING STARTED

Graham chose a rich red colour to decorate the room and this was the starting point. As the dark carpet was to remain, pale furnishings were required to lift the scheme.

DESIGNER'S INSPIRATION BOARD

Graham felt that the room needed a simple, classical style of decoration in a colour that would have traditionally been used in a room of this period and scale. Victorian decorators often combined expensive Crimson pigment with deeper shades of Burnt Sienna and a small amount of Blue pigment to produce a deep red.

It seemed to Graham that the whole room was 'upside down'. To have a dark green ceiling with dark green walls down to dado height then cream from dado to skirting made it appear stunted. Graham wanted to paint the walls in one colour to visually heighten them and to use light tones on the ceiling to reflect natural light back into the room. Interest on the walls could be achieved by painting stripes from picture rail to skirting in a burgundy red using a scumble paint finish to add texture.

Heavy swags and tails were replaced by deep bullion fringing and the formal curtains were turned inside out to reveal their parchment lining, then trimmed with bullion fringing.

PAINTING THE CEILING

First of all, the carpet was covered up. The original skirtings, cornice and window frames were left white and the ceiling was emulsioned (we used Brilliant White 'Once'):

■ Work off a ladder and use a roller to cover the ceiling with paint. Cut in with a 2.5cm (1in) brush.

A formal approach seemed to be the best scheme to follow in this room. A dark red was used with contrasting creams for a traditional look.

CREATING STRIPED WALLS

Emulsion was applied on the walls, picture rail and frieze (we used Crimson) and then burgundy stripes were added:

▪ Work with a roller, cutting in with a 2.5cm (1in) brush. One coat of paint should be sufficient coverage and this will dry in an hour. If the paint appears patchy, apply a second coat.

CHECKLIST

DAY ONE:

- Clear room and protect carpet
- Emulsion ceiling
- Apply the base and stripes to walls
- Make ottoman
- Sew bullion fringing to curtains and track
- Make radiator cover

DAY TWO:

- Upholster ottoman
- Make chair runners
- Make cushions and tablecloth
- Decoupage light shades
- Paint lamp bases and radiator cabinet
- Make fake topiary and painting
- Marble plant holders

Lighter-coloured pictures and lampshades (left) became more prominent when set against the deep red walls. A traditional plaster recess (below) was filled with foliage that was gathered from the garden.

▪ Drop a plumb line from the picture rail to the floor and use this line to start masking off the first stripe. Butt two strips of tape together to form a 12.5cm (5in) stripe then drop another plumb line 12.5cm (5in) further down the wall to start a new stripe. Continue until the whole wall is masked off.

▪ Mix a darker shade for the stripes (seven parts paint to three parts glaze – use either scumble glaze or acrylic medium. Our paint mixture was five parts Crimson to two parts Black emulsion.) Mix together in a paint kettle to make a glaze.

▪ Brush the glaze inwards from the tape onto the walls to prevent it from bleeding under the tape. Use 5cm (2in) brushes to create a scumbled, broken texture. Dab the still-wet glaze with a dry, soft cloth to soften the paint marks. Leave to dry overnight and then carefully remove the tape.

TRADITIONAL OTTOMAN & CURTAIN FINISH

Once the Victorian look was beginning to take shape, Graham wanted to use the soft furnishings to introduce classic tailored shapes to lighten the room and add texture and softness.

OTTOMAN

As a practical yet decorative storage solution, Andy and Graham constructed an ottoman from MDF:

■ Measure and cut out the sides, lid and base from MDF with a jigsaw. (We used four pieces of 120 x 30cm/47 x 12in MDF and two pieces of 50 x 30cm/19½ x 12in. The height is 30cm/12in.) Drill and countersink the MDF first, then screw the sides directly together. Screw the base to the underneath of the frame using the 5cm (2in) gap left by the short batten and screw castors and fixings into the base.

■ Cut a piece of 7.5cm (3in) foam to the same size as the lid and fix this over the lid with double-sided tape. Staple upholstery wadding over the sides of the lid (staple to the outside edge of the frame). Another piece of wadding is stretched over the foam on the lid and stapled to the underside. Staple the centre of the wadding and progress towards each corner.

■ Staple cotton duck canvas over the wadding, keeping the staples to the

MATERIALS & EQUIPMENT

Retractable tape measure and pencil
6mm (¼in) MDF (see instructions for the required amount)
2.5 x 2.5cm (1 x 1in) MDF (we used 25cm/10in)
Jigsaw
Power drill fitted with wood drill bit
Power screwdriver
Short wood screws
Small furniture castors and fixings
Dressmaking scissors

7.5cm (3in) foam (cut to the same size as your lid)
Double-sided masking tape
Staple gun
Upholstery wadding
Cotton duck canvas (400g/14oz flame-retardant)
2 large flush hinges
Small screwdriver
Upholstery cord (we used 3½m/11ft)
Curved needle and upholstery thread

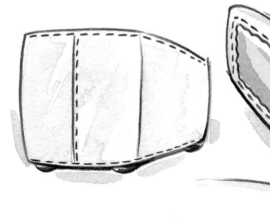

inside edges. Cover the sides using two pieces of the fabric, overlapping the edges neatly on the two shorter sides. Pull the fabric over the lid tightly to flatten the square sides of the foam and staple on the inside of the lid. Use flush hinges to secure the lid to the box. Finally, handstitch upholstery cord around the lid base.

TRIMMING THE CURTAINS

The existing curtains were traditionally sewn with a handstitched goblet pleat heading. Graham removed the hooks and replaced them on the other side of the curtain so that the ivory lining was to the front. The swags and tails were removed and replaced with bullion fringing stapled onto the old pelmet rail:

■ Remove the hooks. For a regular tape heading, flatten out the gathered heading by unfastening the cords and sewing a new heading tape to the other side without removing the original. Handstitch fringing onto the leading edge of the curtain and across the hem at the base to disguise the lining edge.
■ Finally, make tie backs from purchased cord and staple bullion fringing over the pelmet.

CREATING THE CHAIR RUNNERS

Other soft furnishings introduced into the room included chair 'runners':
■ Take the fabric (we used about 2.5m/8ft of linen and silk union) up from the floor, up and over the seat cushion, back rest and chair to hit the flooring on the other side. (The width is the chair width.) Stitch the fabric along its width 5cm (2in) from the top and bottom. Create 5cm (2in) fringing by teasing out the weft threads (stop at the stitching line).

Cushions and tablecloths (above) are a simple way to alter a room. Hem a square of fabric for the tablecloth and make coordinating cushions (see page 62). The cream-coloured ottoman (right) was practical and decorative.

PUTTING THE LOOK TOGETHER

To continue the elegant feel of the room, Graham decided to introduce some classic finishing touches. Topiary trees framed the beautiful bay window and parchment lights decorated the marbled mantlepiece.

Photocopies were elegantly framed and also used as decoupage motifs to decorate the parchment lampshades.

DECOUPAGED LIGHTSHADES

The lampshades were decoupaged with black and white images and the wooden bases were given a paint treatment:

■ Cut out your images, apply spray mount to the back, then place on the shade. Seal with acrylic satin varnish applied with a 2.5cm (1in) brush and leave to dry for about an hour.

■ Key the base with fine-grade sand-paper. Stipple matt black paint with a 2.5cm (1in) brush and leave to dry for an hour.

■ Mix a bronze pigment together (we used one part black carbon powder, one part 'bronze base' and one part micro-crystalline wax). Combine the pigment with an old 2.5cm (1in) brush and use the brush to apply this over the base. After ten minutes, buff the surface up with a soft cloth.

RADIATOR COVERS

Andy constructed radiator covers from 18mm (¾in) MDF. To make your own:

■ Measure the height, width and depth of the radiator and add on 15cm (6in) all round. Cut out two sides and the cover front. Draw a box on the front cover for the opening, 10cm (4in) in from all four sides. Drill a pilot hole and cut out the centre area with a jigsaw.

■ Drill pilot holes and use small wood screws to secure the MDF fretwork to the back of the smaller rectangles. Screw

MDF fretwork (we used 5 x 30cm/2 x 12in) centrally behind the outer panels along the top inside frame edges and repeat along the bottom inside edges to hold the smaller panel. Repeat the process for the central panel.

■ Assemble the front and sides together with small fixing blocks screwed to the inside corners. Use the same fixing blocks to screw the frame to the wall.

■ Cut a shelf to overhang the frame by about 2cm (1in). Panel-pin this to the frame, pre-drilling small pilot holes first. Cut and mitre lengths of moulding and use panel adhesive and panel pins to

Above: Clever accessorizing in shades of cream helped to offset the formal deep red colours used in the room to great effect.

secure this neatly to the shelf. Fix skirting board to both the front and sides.

▪ Fill any holes with all-purpose filler and smooth with sandpaper when dry (about 20 minutes). Prime and leave to dry for two hours. Apply a top coat of white eggshell paint using a 7.5cm (3in) brush and cut in where necessary. Leave to dry overnight. Paint the fretwork grilles in the same way as the lampshade base. Screw magnetic catches to the radiator inside and to the inside of the front panel so that the front is removable for easy access to the radiator controls.

FINISHING TOUCHES

Topiary trees were created by pushing box tree sprigs into a chicken wire ball, wrapped around an oasis block, and this was secured to a thick, rustic wooden pole (use a slim tree trunk as an alternative). The pole was fixed into the planter with a plaster of Paris mix. Painted swirls of artist's oil colours (Crimson and Burnt Sienna) simulated marbling on the planters. Finally, Graham added some cushions, pictures (he adapted a line drawing by projecting it onto a stretched canvas and traced off over the outline with thinned acrylic paint) and filled vases with bunches of foliage that were gathered from the garden.

bloomsbury BEDROOM

Sue and Nigel had a spare room in their large, four-bedroomed property that was, quite frankly, a bit of a tip. They knew it too but they only had this room in which to store all the bits and pieces that one would normally keep in an attic, garage or cellar. Sue had tried to disguise bulging storage racks with rattan roller blinds fixed over the front of the shelves and had draped fringed scarves to cover cardboard boxes in an attempt to make the room pleasant. It was, after all, sometimes used as a spare room so it needed to be comfortable.

I worked in the room with Rav and Michelle, Sue and Nigel's neighbours, and they wanted to reorganize the space completely and to remove the clutter. Rav was keen on concealed storage but everything still needed to be completely accessible. Nigel used this room as a work-room so the furnishings needed to be kept to a minimum, with easy-to-maintain surfaces.

Michelle wanted to use strong colours and paint effects. She showed me Sue and Nigel's bedroom which was painted in a bright jade green proving that they would definitely not be horrified by a strong palette. I was also inspired by the bold pictures that were displayed in other rooms in the house. Nigel collected limited edition prints by several well known artists. The room was such a blank canvas that I borrowed references from other rooms and was inspired by colours taken from a fine art print.

Right: The room was almost collapsing under the strain of boxes and crates as it was used as a storage area. However, with a little imagination, it also became a spare room (left).

GETTING STARTED

A recent visit to Charleston, gathering place of the Bloomsbury set of artists and writers, inspired this room. Charleston is uniquely adorned with colours, textures and paints.

DESIGNER'S INSPIRATION BOARD

I loved the amalgamation of colours used for decorating at Charleston. In the studio there, the walls are not painted with simply one colour but many different shades, with contrasting colour strips in one corner. The treatment, I thought, would also work well in this room. I decided to construct a huge storage unit that looked like a false wall when you entered the room. Behind the wall would be shelves of varying proportions reaching from floor level to ceiling height. This would solve the entire problem of storage in the room (and possibly across the whole house).

I wanted to use separate colours for painting the walls and another colour for painting the ceiling. More importantly, I wanted to decorate the false wall with a naive form of flower painting, using painted panels influenced by Charleston. The room needed more furniture but despite a search around the house, I didn't find anything suitable. Luckily I managed to get some bargains at a local junk shop. I bought two drawer and cupboard units, a three-armed candlelabra and a coffee table.

SANDING & PAINTING THE FLOORBOARDS

Once the carpet was removed, the first priority was to sand and then paint the floorboards (see page 130):

■ Mix together acrylic wood dye (we used about a quarter of a small tin of Dewberry) and add the same amount of white emul-

An eclectic mix of colours, patterns and textures was the starting point for the overall design of this room. I used toning colours right across the spectrum for an individual look.

CHECKLIST

DAY ONE:

- Clear room
- Remove carpet
- Sand floor
- Paint and varnish floor
- Paint walls and ceiling
- Jigsaw drawer and cupboard units and reassemble into armoire cupboard
- Cut pediment for top of armoire
- Sand armoire, apply base coat and decorate
- Revamp small junk table
- Prepare shutters for windows
- Sew bedspread

DAY TWO:

- Paint and fix shelves into alcove
- Build 'T' shaped storage wall
- Fit shelves into construction
- Decorate shelves and storage wall
- String paper and wooden beads together to make radiator cover
- Fit shelf above radiator
- Paint radiator and surround
- Hang beaded trim and fix MDF panels over radiator
- Paint candlelabra
- Replace bed with new truckle bed

■ Tip a matchpot of one colour into a paint kettle. Add the same amount of cold tap water. Stir well.

■ Use a 10cm (4in) brush to apply the colour over the walls. Brush outwards in all directions. (We used Empire Gold on most of the walls but the walls behind the storage unit were painted in Etruscan Red.) Leave to dry for one hour.

PAINTING THE CEILING

We roller-painted a mixture of one part Blue Velvet to one part White paint in a solid colour across the whole ceiling.

The floorboards were colour washed using a thin blue wash which allowed the wood tones to show through. A green chenille rug softened the floor and collections of wickerwork looked interesting against the walls.

sion paint and tap water. Mix together well with a paintbrush. Use a 10cm (4in) brush to sweep colour quickly over the boards in the direction of the grain.

■ Leave to dry for an hour, then protect and seal the boards with two coats of acrylic floor varnish. Allow the first coat to dry (leave for an hour before applying the second), then leave the floorboards overnight to dry completely.

COLOUR WASHING THE WALLS

The skirtings, window frames and architraves were left off-white but matt emulsion (Etruscan Red and Empire Gold) was used on the walls:

CLEVER STORAGE IDEAS

Storage solutions were a big part of this room and while the concealed storage area could cope with most of the items, the room needed some interesting furniture.

ELEGANT ARMOIRE

An armoire was made from two pieces of furniture: one with a high cupboard but small drawers and the other with deeper drawers but a small cupboard:

▪ Jigsaw the pieces into two then fix the deeper drawers from one piece to the larger cupboard and sand.

▪ Screw the two parts together at sides, back and front. Use leftover timber to make a broken pediment on top of the cupboard. Work out the length by measuring the width and depth of the cupboard. Draw a rectangle of these dimensions onto lining paper. Cut out and fold in half. Draw one half of the pediment and the other is a mirror image. Transfer onto timber using carbon paper.

▪ Cut out the pediment (Andy used a router for a really shaped finish). Smooth with sandpaper. Cut sides for the return edges and screw these onto the cupboard top with fixing blocks. Sand and apply white spray primer which dries in five minutes then apply a base and top coat. Leave to dry for one hour.

▪ Decorate freehand style with matchpots, replace the handles and varnish.

MATERIALS & EQUIPMENT

2 junk drawer and cupboard units
Jigsaw and router
Power sander
Medium-grade sandpaper
Short wood screws
Power screwdriver
Retractable tape measure
Pencil and lining paper
Scissors
Carbon paper
Fixing blocks (we used 5cm/2in)

White spray primer
Base coat emulsion (we used Snowflake)
7.5cm (3in) brushes
Matt emulsion paint (we used Golden Meadow)
Artist's bristle brushes
Matchpots of paint (we used Etruscan Red and Livery)
Replacement handles
Spray polyurethane varnish

TERRACOTTA SHELVING

Andy fitted the alcove area with shelves, colour washed in the same terracotta as used on the walls. (See page 151.)

SCREENED STORAGE AREA

Andy resolved storage problems with a useful area that also became an attractive feature of the room:

■ Measure the available space to determine the storage area. Use two timber rectangle shapes cut from 5 x 5cm (2 x 2in) timber to make a frame. Fit one rectangle inside the other for a 'T' shape. Cut an angle from one corner to go over the cornice and cut out the square corner. Replace with a diagonal section. Screw the framework to the ceiling, walls and floor.

■ The longer cross section needs cross bars across the centre sections. The frame is lifted into place and screwed onto the centre section and to the floor and ceiling. Measure the partition inside and outside the framework and square up to decide the coverage. Nail the board over the frame with plasterboard nails. Use a plasterboard shaver to remove any rough edges or overhang.

■ Cut shelves from 12mm (½in) MDF using batten fixings as for the alcove shelves. Screw each batten into the framework and through the plasterboard. Drop the shelves over the battens, screw into place and paint with a flat matt emulsion (we used Etruscan Red). When dry (about an hour), protect with acrylic varnish, which dries in one hour.

■ Decorate the front of the screen in a similar naïve design to the coffee table.

DECORATING THE COFFEE TABLE
A junk table was painted up in Bloomsbury-style patterning to reflect the design on the screen. (For both of these projects, we used thinned Golden Meadow, Empire Gold, Dewberry, White and Livery matchpots.) Copy the design featured here or experiment with your own ideas.

The false wall was fitted from floor to ceiling with shelves and the small alcove seen here had five narrow shelves to hold delicate linens and decorative ceramics.

PUTTING THE LOOK TOGETHER

Sue and Nigel had lots of woven rattan and bamboo artefacts. These worked perfectly to lend a tropical flavour to the decoration.

HARLEQUIN SHUTTERS

Shutters were designed to allow light into the room without the need to open them:

■ Measure the window frame and divide into three parts. The wider shutters are equal to one third part each and the smaller ones are each half of the remaining third. Make a wide and small shutter for each window side. Use 7.5 x 2.5cm (3 x 1in) timber for the horizontal sections and 5 x 2.5cm (2 x 1in) timber for the uprights. To fill in the open panels, use 3mm (⅛in) MDF.

■ Rout the timber frame at the edges to fit the MDF (secure with wood glue). Panel-pin lengths of mitred mouldings. Leave to dry for at least two hours.

behind each shape. (Cover staples with braid secured with a hot melt glue gun.)

■ Hinge the screens together, then hinge the two double-panelled screens onto the architrave. Fit magnetic catches at top and bottom of the smallest screens.

BEADED RADIATOR COVER

A radiator at Charleston was covered with macramé and beads. For my version:

■ Wet a paper strip (about 20cm/8in square) with PVA. Wrap the paper around a drinking straw, then remove the straw. Leave to dry thoroughly overnight.

A yellow ochre border (right) was sewn around a faded tea rose fabric panel to make a bedcover. Discs of a similarly patterned fabric decorated the border and these were secured using a close zigzag stitch. The bedcover fitted in well with the style of the armoire and the new shutters at the windows.

■ Divide each panel in half in pencil, mark the centre of each half with a pencil cross and join the outsides together to make diamond shapes at the top and bottom. Drill a pilot hole and insert the cutting blade of the jigsaw, then cut out the diamond shapes. Smooth with medium-grade sandpaper.

■ Dye 2m (7ft) cotton muslin in a hand-wash dye (we used Lilac). Cut the ironed fabric into panels which are then stapled

When you are working to a tight budget, you need to work economically but also imaginatively. This radiator cover (left) is cheap to make and yet the finished effect also looks quite amazing.

■ Make about 120 beads. Fill a plastic bag with beads, pour paint inside and scrunch together. Remove the beads. Dry on a rack (allow an hour). Thread the beads onto string and intersperse the paper beads with wooden ones. Each length is longer than the radiator depth.

■ Fix brackets above the radiator and screw a shelf (cut to the radiator length with 5 x 2.5cm/2 x 1in timber) onto this. Scumble paint the shelf and radiator as the walls. Leave for an hour. Measure the radiator width and divide this into three to decide the position of the diamonds and strings. Cut three rectangles from 12mm (½in) MDF less space for strings in between. Staple four sections of four strings onto the edges under the shelf.

■ Cut diamond shapes in the centre of the radiator cover (leave a 2.5cm (1in) border and paint. Screw the rectangles under the shelf and along a batten screwed to the floor with short wood screws.

FINISHING TOUCHES

Finally, a new 'truckle'-type bed was added, the junk pieces worked well and a chenille rug softened the floorboards.

A wooden candlebra (above) was painted in the same colour as the ceiling and colour washed using a diluted purple emulsion paint.

turquoise BEDROOM

Kate's bedroom in Chiswick is her sanctuary. However, it wasn't as restful or calming as it might have been. A green carpet, with pale walls and mismatched furniture, did little to suggest that this was a haven from the rest of the world.

Graham Wynne, the designer who worked on the room with Kate's neighbours (Charles and Jane) felt that it would benefit from bold, powerful colours. These would not only unify the room but would also make it completely different from the rest of the house. The bedroom was generously proportioned with an attractive bay window and offered enough space for a comfortable seating area. Two large alcoves had fitted wardrobes at either side to provide most of the necessary storage space. Graham was lucky in that several of Kate's belongings – a bed and blanket box made from natural pine – would be easy to decorate. The Edwardian fireplace was in good condition although it needed tender loving care and the roller blinds had the potential for a radical make-over. Jane and Charles told Graham that they wanted to use strong colours but to say that they were a little shocked when the paint lids came off was an understatement. They were speechless as the first layer of colour was rollered over the walls.

Kate's neighbours were keen to make this a room where she could read, relax and feel very comfortable, and somewhere that reflected her own interests.

All the basic elements of a good design were already present in Kate's original scheme (right). The bedroom simply needed to be unified with colour and a certain designer's touch (left).

GETTING STARTED

A strong colour needs an equally powerful shade to provide a balance so by choosing a turquoise paint for the walls, Graham had practically sold himself on Fuchsia Pink.

DESIGNER'S INSPIRATION BOARD

Jane had originally suggested the colour of the sea for Kate's bedroom. She was inspired by the Mediterranean, remembered from past holidays. Jane felt that deep aquatic blue would be appropriate as Kate loves the sea and she had been a crew member on board a yacht for a year. Whilst searching for inspirational blues and greens, Jane and Graham discovered three dramatic sailing pictures that Tim (Kate's lodger) had taken.

The turquoise blue in the photographs was carefully matched on a paint chart by Graham and became the basis of the scheme. He used the principal of complementary colours from the colour wheel. Colours that sit opposite on the wheel, such as purple and yellow, seem to almost vibrate when placed next to one another. Graham deliberately wanted this vibrancy in the scheme of the room. By using a small amount of Fuchsia Pink as a complementary colour, it was possible to achieve a lively interior that needed only cool, crisp white to offset the dramatic turquoise and fuchsia.

SANDING AND PAINTING THE BLEACHED-EFFECT FLOOR

Once the carpet was taken away, Graham, Jane and Charles began the long and arduous task of sanding the floor. Because an electric sander creates so much dust, this kind of preparation should always be done first (see opposite).

Bold contemporary colours need a clean colour to balance and unify the overall effect. Graham introduced elements of white into his design board and this worked really well in the room.

■ Carefully go across the floor space on hands and knees to remove any projecting nail heads and staples with a claw hammer and pliers. Larger nails should be punched below the surface with a hammer and nail punch.

■ Sanders are always supplied in two parts. Start with the large sander and fit it with coarse sandpaper. (Papers will be supplied with the machine. Use in accordance with the manufacturer's instructions.) Work the sander diagonally across the floorboards first of all.

■ Brush away the dust using a vacuum cleaner or dust pan and brush. Once the floorboards are sanded, switch over to a medium-grade sandpaper and sand in the same direction as the boards.

■ Use a smaller, hand-held sander to rub down the edges of the floorboards and to reach into the corners. Remove the dust, wait for about an hour to allow it to settle, then brush away once more.

■ Dilute white acrylic primer with an equal quantity of tap water, then brush this over the floorboards with a wide 7.5cm (3in) brush. Brush each board, following the direction of the grain. Allow about 30 minutes or more for drying. Dip the ends of the same brush into white primer and brush this lightly over the boards to create a streaky effect. Leave to dry for one hour.

■ Seal with two coats of satin varnish. Allow the first coat to dry (about one hour) before applying the second.

PAINTING THE WALLS

The ceiling, coving and skirting were left in their original white. A flat colour (M'Ladies Room), applied with an emulsion roller, was used to cover the walls:

■ Tip a generous amount of paint into a tray and fill the roller by rolling it back-

CHECKLIST

DAY ONE:
• Remove carpet and gripper rods
• Sand, paint and varnish floor
• Paint walls
• Paint blanket box and bed
• Construct new wardrobe doors
• Dye rugs and stitch these together

DAY TWO:
• Paint and wax fireplace
• Construct picture/display frames
• Make table and cloth cover
• Paint blinds and mirror
• Trim and hang muslin drapes
• Spray-paint wicker sofa

wards and forwards in the tray until it is fully charged. Transfer the paint onto the walls and 'cut in' carefully around plug sockets and other features with a smaller 2.5cm (1in) brush. Allow one hour for the paint to dry.

When displayed together in recessed frames like this, smaller objects are given much greater significance.

STORAGE & DISPLAY FEATURES

Graham wanted to keep the wardrobes but to dramatically alter their look. The blanket box would also be retained — he would simply colour wash it, along with some picture frames used as clever storage and display areas.

Small mirrors were secured to the back of these recessed frames to make the display even more effective.

MAKING THE DISPLAY MIRROR FRAMES

These frames are useful for displaying small objects. To make your own:

■ The timber for your frames should be at least 2.5cm/1in in depth. Carefully saw and join each piece using a tenon saw and wood screws.

■ Afix a mirror piece to cover the opening at the back and panel-pin picture molding into place. Decorate with dilute primer (see Wardrobes).

TRANSFORMING THE WARDROBES

Andy gave the tall, thin wardrobes a new look by simply replacing the old doors. The originals had four doors: two larger ones for the lower part and two smaller ones for the top storage area. Two full-length doors were created to fill the space, running from floor to cornice.

■ Unscrew the hinges with a screwdriver. Carefully measure the available space from the top of the kickboard to the bottom of the cornice. Use these measurements to cut a sheet of MDF (see pages 148–9) to size with a jigsaw. With a tape measure and pencil, mark the MDF in half down the centre to divide into two evenly-sized doors.

■ Cut the tongue-and-groove cladding to the same length as the doors and screw onto the fronts. Work from the outside edge inwards and cut away the

MATERIALS & EQUIPMENT

Panel pins and small hammer
Paint kettle and white acrylic primer
7.5cm (3in) brushes
Short wood screws

MIRROR FRAMES
Lengths of timber (2.5cm/1in thick)
Tenon saw
Mirror (cut to size)
Picture moulding

WARDROBES
Large and small screwdrivers

1 x sheet MDF, 1.9cm (¾in)
Jigsaw
Retractable tape measure and pencil
Tongue-and-groove (cut in lengths to cover from floor to ceiling and widths to cover two doors)
Power drill with the wood drill bit
Ready-mixed filler and filler knife
Medium-grade sandpaper
Clear acrylic varnish
Gate-style hinges (Black)
Magnetic catches
Gate-style latches (Black)
Selection of coving

excess at the outside edge using a jigsaw. To secure the tongue-and-groove firmly, screw the timber down every 30cm (12in). Drill a pilot hole first and countersink the hole.

■ Fill the holes with all-purpose filler. Leave to dry for about 20 minutes and then sand with medium-grade sand-paper. Before hanging the doors, apply a coat of dilute white acrylic primer (one part primer to an equal amount of water). Use a wide 7.5cm (3in) brush to apply the primer over the doors following the direction of the wood grain. Leave to dry, then streak as for the floor. Protect and seal the surface with a coat of clear matt acrylic varnish. This should dry in about an hour.

■ Hang the doors with the heavy gate-style hinges allowing the longest part of the hinge to appear on the front of the door. Fix magnetic catches on the inside of the doors with a small screwdriver. Finally, to complete the look, add gate-style latches to match the hinges. Use the hammer to panel-pin a piece of coving across the top of the cupboard for a neater finish.

WHITEWASHED BLANKET BOX
Both the bed and blanket box were whitewashed using a dilute solution of white acrylic primer in the same way as the floor. The lacquered pine surface was first lightly keyed with a medium-grade sand-paper block and then an inter-esting patchy effect was created with the thinned primer and sealed with a coat of clear matt acrylic varnish.

Graham used a small pot of Treasure Silver gilding wax, applied with the fingertips, to highlight the raised details of the elegant fire surround.

PUTTING THE LOOK TOGETHER

Once the strong colour theme had been decided, then everything else in the room was adapted to fit in with this. Flashes of crisp white pulled the whole scheme together.

The soft colour of the floorboards was echoed in the picture frames, on the bed, wardrobe doors and blanket box. Continuing the theme, solid white was used for the muslin curtains, bedcover and table and blanket box.

SIMPLY-STYLED TABLE & CALICO CLOTH

For the low table, Graham needed an inexpensive base. Four lengths of 5 x 5cm (2 x 2in) timber were used with a rectangle of MDF cut to size by Andy for the tabletop (see pages 148–9).

■ Screw the top onto the legs with long wood screws keeping the edge of the legs flush to the table edge. Cross-brace the sides with lengths of 12.5 x 2.5cm (5 x 1in) timber screwed between each leg using long wood screws.

■ Use white cotton calico to make the tablecloth. Measure the table from the floor across the width and then measure the length in the same way adding 5cm (2in) all round for a seam allowance. Cut the fabric to size and turn under the raw edges using the seam allowance. Press and throw the cover over the table, folding the corners underneath. Handsew two cotton ties one third of the way down from the top of the table to neaten the cloth.

MAKING THE BLINDS

Kate's blinds were adapted to work with the rest of the scheme:

■ Remove the blinds from their fixings and lay flat on a work surface. Dilute pink dye with about ten times as much water. This will produce a pale pink colour if it is applied to white or cream blinds. Wash colour over the blind.

■ Once the paint is dry (allow one hour), mark 5cm (2in) lines across the length of the blind. Place masking tape along the lines to form stripes. Use neat fabric dye to paint in the pink stripes. Brush inwards from the tape to prevent the colour from seeping through. Allow at least one hour for the paint to dry then remove the masking tape.

The new wicker seating (right) was sprayed with white car spray paint to soften the original honey colour and brightly coloured cushions were quickly made up (see page 62).

MUSLIN & RIBBON DRAPES

Sew white ribbon ties to the top of ready-made muslin drapes and tie these onto metal curtain poles fixed above the blinds. Three straight poles above each window created the 'bay' shape.

FUCHSIA FLOORING

Graham dyed three smaller rugs separately and stitched them together with turquoise thread.

■ Use one box of machine dye (we used Deep Pink) for each rug. Follow the manufacturer's instructions and leave to dry before sewing the rugs together.

FINISHING TOUCHES

Kate's mirror frame was whitewashed to match the bed and blanket box. To harmonize with this, wicker furniture was sprayed with white car paint, while floating candles added a romantic touch.

Church candles were placed on either side of the mirror and a candle on the mantlepiece illuminated this area. Two table lamps added to the ambience.

The bedroom looked quite different at the end of the two days. Kate had never suspected that her neighbours would have chosen such dramatic colours but she loved the warm and restful result.

Kate's oval mirror was rehung lengthways and two metal candle sconces were screwed to the wall on either side above the fireplace.

mexican KITCHEN

Hot, powerful colours were once again on the agenda. Kate and Tim wanted to use a rich blue with a strong colour wash for the walls in their neighbours' kitchen. With this in mind, my thoughts turned towards Mexico. I suggested blue cupboards and terracotta for the walls – and how would they feel about punched tin?

Charles is a passionate cook and there was so much about the old kitchen that prevented him from doing this well, with interrupted work areas being the biggest problem. The tall fridge-freezer unit was badly placed and if this was moved to the other end of the kitchen he would have a complete run of work surface. If I repositioned two wall units above this area then all the cooking ingredients would be to hand. After measuring up, this proved to be an extremely practical solution. There was space for a base unit and I decided to move the dishwasher. Charles would be left with the perfect work area and he would also have a spacious cooking area. There were two other fixtures that I wanted to retain but needed to paint and these were the dresser and small shelving unit. The shelving unit posed no problems at all but Kate was more anxious about painting Jane's new pine dresser – 'Would the paint come off easily if they didn't like it?' 'Well, not without a great deal of work,' I told her but it would look so good once it was painted and waxed in the same way as the cupboard units, and so she let me go ahead with my plans.

Left: A far cry from the clinical white units and pale walls of the original scheme (right), Jane and Charles wondered if they were in the right house when they first saw their vibrantly coloured kitchen.

GETTING STARTED

The Mexican theme was a great starting point as it not only gave us the basic blue and terracotta palette but also licence to use a whole range of colours and intricate decorations.

DESIGNER'S INSPIRATION BOARD

Fortunately, I had some close friends who had travelled to Mexico and looking through their books, china and tinware certainly provided a wealth of inspirational details. Tiny Mexican figurines were characteristically decorated with fine, cross-hatched penwork that I transferred around the edge of the kitchen table. Punched tin is typically Mexican and although it would have been impossible to punch all of the cupboard panels, we would at least have the time to punch two of them leaving the others as plain.

As I was not content just to leave the blue of the units and dresser as a flat colour, I encouraged Tim and Kate to wipe a layer of coloured wax over the surface to age it and knock back the intensity of the colour.

In addition to all this, a lizard motif was cut out of a wooden bench and small tin vessels gave the true flavour of a Mexican cantina.

ADDING A WORKTOP

Once the dishwasher had been replumbed (by joining the pipework close to the washing machine), the kitchen was cleared and wall cupboards removed. We then added a new worktop section:

■ Secure the worktop (measured and cut to size) to the back of the wall with a metal bracket and prop by resting it on the unit carcass and new MDF side. Use a chrome joining strip to neaten rough edges.

Kate and Tim were keen to use bold colours in the kitchen. The combination of blue and terracotta was successful on the design board and so I was looking forward to seeing it in the kitchen.

PREPARING THE WALLS

The wallpaper was stripped and the kitchen walls were painted:

◼ A hired steam stripper will make the work of stripping walls easier. Score the surface of the wallpaper with the edge of a screwdriver or craft knife to allow steam to penetrate through the paper and to remove it more quickly.

◼ Sand the walls (a hired sander is easiest) and then apply the colour wash with a 10cm (4in) brush (we used Flambeau mixed one to one with water). (The ceiling and skirtings were left Magnolia.)

LAYING THE VINYL FLOORING

We removed part of the old lino and replaced it with an offcut of solid blue vinyl. To calculate the amount of vinyl that you will need:

◼ Measure the longest width of the floor and then measure the longest length of floor area. Multiply the figures together.

◼ Unscrew any brass treads and pull up the flooring. If this is too stubborn to remove, fix new flooring on top of the old.

◼ Make a template for the new vinyl (cut this out from

Although Kate was initially worried about painting the dresser, she was thrilled with the finished effect.

the original flooring or lay sheets of newspaper over the area, joining them with masking tape) to cut out the correct shape. Clean the sub-floor well with a kitchen floor cleaner and then lay strips of double-sided carpet tape across the floor area.

◼ Lay the vinyl over the top of the surface starting with a corner or straight edge first. Press the vinyl down with your hands, replace treads as necessary and fit any excess under the kickboards.

CHECKLIST

DAY ONE:
- Plumb dishwasher
- Move fridge-freezer
- Fix new top over dishwasher
- Strip wallpaper and prepare walls
- Paint walls terracotta
- Remove flooring and lay new vinyl
- Remove and reposition wall units
- Assemble fronts for cupboard doors
- Saw MDF for unit doors
- Start to prime, paint and wax doors
- Cut and punch two tin panels
- Paint shelving unit and dresser

DAY TWO:
- Complete cupboard doors
- Make up and decorate bench seat
- Sew Roman blinds
- Fix wooden battens and hang blinds
- Cut tabletop, secure legs, paint and apply varnish

PUNCHED TIN CUPBOARDS

An antiqued blue paint finish was combined with punched tin on two of the wall units to evoke the feeling of a traditional Mexican room.

The tin on the other wall units was left unpunched, but the same paint finish was applied. To make the panels:

■ With a screwdriver, remove the doors from the base unit keeping the hinge mechanism on the door frame. Measure each door and cut MDF into 6cm (2.5in) strips. Remember that each strip starts about 1cm (⅜in) in from the edge.

■ Use butt joints (see page 150) to secure the MDF allowing the two longer sides to be cut to full length and the shorter sides are fitted in between. Drill and countersink two holes on each MDF strip. Fix with panel adhesive to the door panel front and screw from inside.

■ Cut a sheet of zinc to the same size as the door, less 5cm (2in) all round, using tin snips.

■ Key the outside edges of the doors (about 5cm/2in) all round with sandpaper, then prime the doors and MDF strips. Leave to dry for one hour.

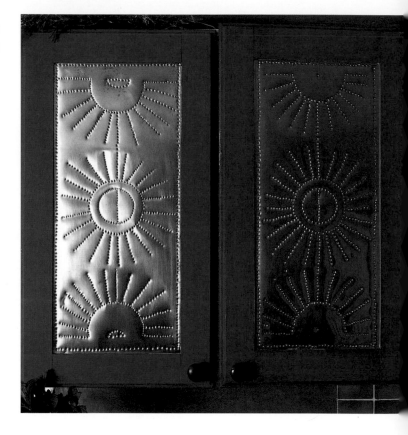

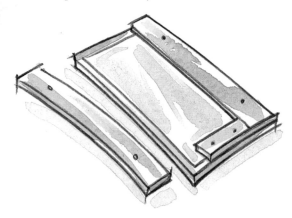

■ Apply panel adhesive over the door and press the zinc sheets (see opposite) on top of the MDF. Press down firmly to create a strong bond. This will be firm in a few minutes and dry after an hour or so. Use short wood screws to fix each strip into place.

■ Fill the holes with ready-mixed surface filler using a filler knife. When dry (about 30 minutes), smooth down with fine grade sandpaper and apply a base coat of matt emulsion. This will be dry after about an hour.

■ Wipe liquid wax over the base coat using a pad of medium-grade wire wool. Replace the handles.

■ Rescrew the panels then screw long wood screws through the back panels.

Although it can be quite time consuming, the finished result of punched tin is very effective. These two panels on the kitchen wall units (above) were decorated with bold, geometric patterns. The lizard cut-out featured on the storage chest (right) is a traditionally popular Mexican motif.

CREATING THE PUNCHED TIN EFFECT

The tin was inspired by an authentic Mexican cabinet.

▪ Lay zinc sheeting on a piece of scrap timber, then place this over a flat work surface. Find the centre of the zinc (measure the width and mark the middle, then do the same with the length and draw up a dividing point) and mark this with a wax crayon. Place a circular guide over the mark (we used a roll of masking tape and drew around this with crayon).

▪ Use a ruler to draw radiating spikes (about 5cm/2in long) from the edge of the exterior ring. Mark out two half circles at the top and bottom of the

MATERIALS & EQUIPMENT

Screwdriver
Kitchen cupboard doors
Retractable tape measure
Pencil
Jigsaw
6mm (¼in) MDF
Drill with wood drill bit
Countersink drill bit
Panel adhesive
Short wood screws
Zinc sheeting
Tin snips and protective gloves
Fine-grade sandpaper
White acrylic primer
7.5cm (3in) and 2.5cm (1in) brushes

Surface filler and filler knife
Matt emulsion (we used Blue Pencil)
Liquid wax (Dark Oak)
Medium-grade wire wool
Handles (we sprayed the originals
   with plasticote spray enamel)

PUNCHED TIN EFFECT
Wax crayon
Masking tape
Ruler
Flat-headed nail
Medium-weight hammer
Pad of steel wool
Methylated spirits

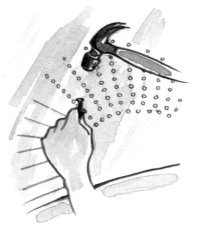

panel (use the exterior of the masking roll). Draw out the radiating lines until they almost touch the previous lines. You may need to alter your measurements to accommodate the dimensions of your panels.

▪ Take a flat-headed nail and a hammer and use this to punch out the design following the crayon guidelines. Keep the distance between each of the punched holes as even as possible. Punch around the edges of the panels too. Wipe away marks with a pad of steel wool that has been soaked in methylated spirits.

LIZARD STORAGE CHEST
Andy transformed a simple wooden chest into a storage bench by adding a shaped back and sides to the unit. He cut a lizard motif out of the centre panel using a jigsaw. The unit was then colour washed (we used Pencil Blue) and sealed with varnish.

PUTTING THE LOOK TOGETHER

We uncovered some brightly-coloured earthenware from Jane's collection of pottery and stripped bunches of herbs from the garden to hang from metal butcher's hooks.

PINE SHELVING

A simple but effective paint treatment, using the same warm terracotta shade as the walls, revamped the pine shelving:

■ Sand the shelving and wash it over with thinned emulsion (we used the same one as for the walls, one part paint/water).

■ When the paint is dry, spray with varnish.

The same thinned terracotta wall wash is used to transform an old pine shelving rack (above). A coat of varnish protects the finished colour. A clever combination of tin kitchen utensil holders, bold, bright painted colours on the table and checkered Roman blinds (above right) brings the look together.

CHECKERED ROMAN BLINDS

We made some Roman blinds from heavy Indian cotton:

■ Measure the width and length of the windows. Decide whether the blind is to hang inside or outside any window recess (outside the recess requires a little more fabric). Add 5cm (3in) to this all round for turnings and hem.

■ To give characteristically crisp folds to the blinds, separate rod pockets were made for each dowelling rod at the top of the blinds. Each pocket is made from 7.5cm (3in) width strips cut to the length of the blind plus 5cm (2in) for seam allowances. Press the longest raw edges underneath using the smallest turning. Fold these together. Fold under one of the shorter edges, press and sew around three sides. Construct three pockets for the long kitchen window blind.

■ With the wrong side of the blind facing you, divide the drop into eight equal parts. Pin one rod pocket three-eighths of the way down from the top

of the blind, another pocket two eighths down from this and a third pocket two eighths down from the second. The flap at the bottom of the blind should measure the final eighth. Stitch across the top of each rod pocket keeping close to the raw edges.

■ Sew one part of a touch-and-close fastener to the top of the blind and staple the second part to a wooden 5 x 2.5cm (2 x 1in) batten. (To fix the batten, screw two eyelets at the base, one 7.5cm/3in from either end.) Sew blind rings at either end of the rod

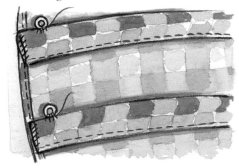

pockets using small handstitches (longer blinds will need centre blind rings). Push 9mm (^{3}⁄$_8$in) dowelling into each pocket. Tie blind cord to the lower rings and pass this through the rings and eyelets. Pass the cords to one side.

■ Press the fastener together, tie the cords and hold with a cleat.

MULTI-COLOURED TABLETOP

An MDF tabletop was painted with leaf motifs and a Mexican pattern:

■ Cut a half sheet of 1.9cm (¾in) MDF to size (see pages 148–9). Sand the edges and use short wood screws to fix four purchased table legs underneath, about 10cm (4in) in from the corners.

■ Prime and leave to dry for about an hour. Decorate freehand using match-pots. When dry (after about an hour), seal with two coats of spray varnish. Allow half an hour between coats.

FINISHING TOUCHES

The pine dresser was moved into the gap between the fridge-freezer and the cooking area and it looked great when it was painted using the same technique as for the kitchen units.

Coloured ceramics, vases, urns and a candlelabra were all displayed on shelves and surfaces and these really helped to authenticate the Mexican style.

Charles and Jane were thrilled with their new look Mexican kitchen. The room seemed so different that they were quite shocked and amazed to discover that they really were back at home in their own kitchen.

A hanging rack was removed from the hallway and used to hold kitchen utensils and herbs above the cooker.

practical advice

This section of the book is a useful and practical guide for anyone who wishes to recreate some of the rooms outlined in this book. Here we show you in detail some of the construction techniques used by Andy on the programme and you will find a quick reference to all the tools, techniques and materials we use.

MATERIALS & EQUIPMENT

However little DIY you do around the home, there is always a hammer, screwdriver or a pot of paint to be found somewhere. Here is a detailed breakdown of a whole range of useful basic equipment, plus some more specialized pieces to help you to complete the projects featured in this book.

PAINTS

Today's paint manufacturers have a huge range of paints and colours. This quick reference guide gives you a clear indication as to what paint is required to get the job done.

PRIMERS

These are available as oil or water-based products. Oil-based primer is suitable for preparing stone, concrete, wood, chipboard, hardboard and ply-wood. Acrylic primer is water-soluble and used on soft and hard woods, chipboard, hardboard, MDF and plywood.

WATER-BASED PAINTS

For interiors, emulsion is the most commonly-used paint and it is easy to use and quick-drying (most emulsions dry within an hour and brushes are quickly and easily cleaned with water). Special one-coat emulsions are now also available. Cheaper emulsions have poor covering power. Once dry,

the surface is wipe-clean but not washable. These paints are available in a variety of finishes:
- Flat finish or matt emulsions
- Mid sheen finish or vinyl silk or satin emulsions – these paints have a slight sheen and are generally used on walls. They can withstand more cleaning than matt finishes. Water-based gloss paint has been a recent development for use on woodwork.

OIL-BASED PAINTS

These paints are slower-drying than the water-based variety but they are tough and washable. Use white spirit solvent to clean brushes and to dilute paints if necessary. Finishes available include:
- Flat finish (matt) – this looks like an emulsion, but it is an oil-based paint. It is regarded as a specialist product and is only available through certain outlets.
- Mid-sheen finish – known as eggshell paint, it is washable, easy to apply and comes in a wide range of colours. It is sometimes called semi-gloss or satin-wood and may be used on walls and woodwork.
- Gloss finish – a very shiny paint which is generally used on woodwork rather than walls.

VARNISHES

These can be water-based or oil-based and are available in matt, eggshell and gloss finishes. They are also available in spray form. Varnish is used to protect surfaces such as floorboards and gives a lustrous finish that highlights the colour underneath and adds gloss. Oil-based varnishes tend to yellow with age. Water-based varnishes are sufficiently tough and durable to be used on floors with the advantage of being water-soluble. They will not yellow and are quick-drying.

GLAZES

Again, these can be either water or oil-based. They are semi-transparent mediums to which pigment is added. Glaze is painted over a base colour which

It is easy to create a faux stone urn with emulsions, and spray paints were used unconventionally on the chest of drawers (above).

shows through from underneath, particularly when the glaze is broken up with a rag, brush or sponge. It is sometimes called scumble glaze. Most broken paint finishes, colour washing, dragging, stippling, etc. are achieved with a glaze.

ARTIST'S OIL PAINTS

There are two ranges: the more expensive artist's quality which contains the highest grade of materials and student's quality which is cheaper but it is well worth experimenting. Both ranges can only be used with oil-based products.

ARTIST'S ACRYLIC PAINTS

These are pigments which are mixed in an acrylic medium. They are water soluble but dry quickly. Acrylic paints can be used on their own (as for stencilling) or mixed with other water-based paints.

COLOURINGS & PIGMENTS

These are usually artists' products and they are available in both oil and water-based versions. Colourings and pigments are usually mixed in a base before they are applied. Universal stainers can be mixed in water or oil-based paints, glazes or varnishes and they are easy to find in most decorating stores.

BRUSHES

Natural products such as bristle or hair, as well as artificial fibres, are used to make brushes. There are many types on the market but the following types of brushes should see you through most of the *Changing Rooms* makeovers:

■ Decorator's brushes – walls, woodwork and plaster surfaces are usually painted with ordinary decorators' flat-bristled brushes. For awkward areas, such as window frames and architraves (and also for cutting in), always use the smaller thicknesses of brush (anything from 1cm/¼in to 5cm/2in). Flatter wall surfaces require 7.5cm (3in) to 10–12½cm (4–5in) brushes.

■ Stencilling brushes – these have short, stiff bristles which are cut flat at the ends. They are ideal for stippling paint through a stencil.

■ Artist's brushes – these are available in a variety of shapes and sizes and in all manner of different materials. Generally, on the programme we tend to use stiff-bristled brushes with either pointed or chisel-shaped ends.

ROLLERS

The advantage of using rollers is the speed in which an area can be covered. When working on a smooth surface, use a short pile roller; on a textured surface, you will find that a roller with a medium pile is best and a heavily textured surface requires a long pile.

Be careful not to overload the roller (this is a common mistake) as the paint will spray everywhere, splattering both the paint surface and your skin. Use a sloping ribbed tray to avoid this. Fill the tray one third full of paint, dip in the roller and then roll it over the ribs to evenly distribute the paint. Clean the roller in warm, soapy water and hang it up to dry. If you have to stop work for a short time, place the roller in a plastic bag to prevent the paint from drying out.

BASIC TECHNIQUES

When decorating an interior, there is a practically limitless choice of paints, techniques and effects that can be done. Here are a few of the techniques available to you which we have featured in the rooms in this book.

BASIC PREPARATION

Surface preparation can often take longer than actual decoration but good preparation ensures that the paint stays where it should be – on the wall! Sugar soap is perfect for washing down painted woodwork prior to re-painting. Other surfaces are more usually prepared with sandpaper. A light sanding over a painted or varnished surface will 'key' the surface.

COLOUR WASHING

Uneven brush strokes form part of the overall effect of this simple paint technique. For a rustic effect, choose a dark coloured emulsion and dilute this with anything from equal parts water to paint to up to nine parts water to one part paint (see page 139). To achieve a softer effect, use scumble glaze with paint to create a cloudy look (see pages 98–9). A dark colour wash (apply with a 10–12.5cm/4–5in brush) works well over a pale base coat. Depending on the effect, usually only a single layer of colour wash is applied over a good base.

FRESCO EFFECT

This technique was featured on the first *Changing Rooms* programme (see page 36). Basically, it uses the colour wash technique but rather than just one colour, three layers are applied to build up a cloudy, layered effect.

Left, above and right: Here, similar results are produced by using thinned emulsion paints to create interesting, colour washed effects.

ANTIQUING

This effect is seen on a number of surfaces throughout the book and it is ideal for simulating an aged effect.

WAX DISTRESSING

This antiquing effect is perhaps the simplest one of all (see page 85). An ordinary household candle is applied to a dry coat of coloured emulsion and then a top layer of paint is applied. Once dry, the surface is rubbed with sandpaper to reveal the base.

SOFT WAX DISTRESSING

Similar to wax distressing, in this case a softer furniture wax is applied over the first (dry) coat of emulsion with a paintbrush or soft cloth. A second layer of paint is applied and once dry, a cloth is used to wipe away excess paint and wax for a softer effect.

ANTIQUING WITH WAX

Not to be confused with distressed finishes, this technique uses coloured furniture wax applied with a wire wool pad over the dried paint surface (see page 35). The painted surface deepens its colour once the wax is applied and the wax will also protect the underlying surface.

MASKING OFF FOR STRIPES

We often use low-tack masking tape to produce stripes of colour over a painted surface (see page 115). Low-tack masking tape is far less tacky than regular and is less likely to damage the underlying painted surface. When painting stripes or lines, always feather the paint inwards from each side of the tape to prevent paint from seeping underneath.

PAINTING FLOORS

Because of the time pressures that we face when filming *Changing Rooms*, we tend to favour water-based products as these are quicker-drying and also much easier to apply (particularly in the case of walls and floors). When painting prepared floors with a water-based product, leave it to dry thoroughly (allow one to two hours) before a protective coat of

Antique finishes can be used on old surfaces such as the fireplace (left) to enhance original details and they work equally well on contemporary panelling (as above).

varnish is applied (leave overnight). Water-based varnish is popular because of its shorter drying time.

WAXING FLOORS

Wax can be applied over prepared wooden floorboards (see page 27). It should be applied with brushes (the shoe cleaning type) or soft cloths and then buffed up to a low sheen. Leave the wax to dry for a few hours or preferably overnight before buffing to a sheen.

HANDY ANDY'S
hints & tips

Handy Andy, he's the designer's guardian angel. He offers advice (sometimes unwanted) on what is achievable and what isn't. Whenever we need someone to create the unusual or to repair the unsightly or just to cover up the unmentionable, he's there. Often it's with a characteristic quip of uninvited comment but always with practical, down-to-earth advice. We'd be lost without him. Here are some of his basic hints and tips:

EQUIPMENT & GENERAL TECHNIQUES

Most of the equipment that we use can be found in any DIY-minded person's tool kit. A few pieces are sometimes needed for more specialist jobs and these can be hired.

ROUTERS

An electric tool that is used to cut grooves and recesses. It is particularly useful for shaping timber and MDF for decorative mouldings. There are various cutting bits which are interchangeable and these give different sizes and shapes of finish. A router is mainly used for shaping whereas a jigsaw is mostly used for cutting.

POWER SANDERS

Orbital sanders are great when you need to sand flat areas but the abrasive paper that you need to attach to the machine always moves in tiny circles so finish your sanding off by hand, following in the direction of the wood grain. Power sanders are available in a variety of sizes.

DRILLS

These are probably the most useful part of any DIY kit. Drills are used for drilling holes for screws or for making large holes in timber and MDF. Specialist interchangeable bits can be used for drilling through metal and masonry.

When drilling into hard masonry, use a drill with a hammer drill option. It is often helpful to withdraw the bit periodically when drilling into wood or metal. You can then remove dust from the drilled hole and this prevents the bit from becoming clogged. For the least damage to a surface, always drill on the most important side. When you want to drill to a certain depth, it is useful to wrap a small amount of coloured tape around the drill bit at the required distance. Drilled holes in timber are often countersunk (the outer edge of the drilled hole is widened) at the top to allow the screw head to be recessed slightly below the surface. Never touch a drill immediately after drilling as they can become very hot.

STAPLE GUNS

A trigger-operated tool which fires a staple straight into the surface. It is very useful for upholstery projects where you are fixing fabric onto timber.

JIGSAWS

When fitted with the correct blade, a jigsaw will cut a variety of materials, either in long, straight lines or in curves, angles and even holes. To jigsaw a straight line, use a pencil and ruler to draw the line first then position the jigsaw blade either to the right or left of this line. For intricate curves, change the regular blade to a narrow profile blade. Gentle curves can be achieved with a regular blade. When cutting curves such as the screen in Belsize Park (see page 38) or an overmantle (see page 87), buy thin profile blades

that have been designed specifically for cutting intricate shapes. Never be tempted to force the jigsaw excessively along the cutting line. It is always best to allow the blade to saw its way through using the minimum of pressure.

MITRE BLOCKS

These are simple frames with slots cut into them at 45 and 90 degrees. Mitre blocks ensure that you can accurately cut timber to make perfect corner joins. To do this, hold the timber in the block and pass your saw through either the 45 degrees or 90 degrees slot. Picture frames should be cut in this way, as should architraves and decorative mouldings.

WORKING WITH GLUES

All-purpose glue will cope with most household repairs. Epoxy and super glues are best for more complicated surfaces and PVA woodworking glue is suitable for general carpentry. Contact adhesive is useful for fabric and vinyl surfaces. Both surfaces need a thin layer of glue and this should be allowed to dry completely before they are bonded together.

> Many solvents are potentially harmful and some are highly inflammable and may give off poisonous fumes. Keep solvents (and all other DIY materials and equipment) away from children and always wear rubber gloves when working with solvents. (See page 154 for more advice on safety.)

HAMMERS

Always hold a hammer near the end and keep your eye on the nail you are about to hit. Start by tapping the nail into the wood, then swing the hammer from your elbow so that the hammer is at right angles to the nail on impact. For light work, use pin hammers and claw hammers are best for heavier projects.

NAILS

A huge variety of nails are available on the market. Choose the right nail for specific projects (most suppliers will be able to advise you). To avoid splitting wood when nailing, blunt the end of the nail with a quick tap from the hammer. When nailing small panel pins, it is sometimes useful to hold these in place with a piece of thin card first.

SCREWDRIVERS & RAWLPLUGS

Many shapes and sizes of screwdriver are available. They vary in the type of tips, shapes of handle and whether they are slotted or crosshead screwdrivers. Ideally, you should have a range of screwdrivers for all sizes of screws.

Several types of rawlplugs are available and the choice depends on the drilled surface. Ask your hardware supplier for advice. The rawlplug should be matched to the drill bit and screw size.

JOINTS

Even on the simplest of DIY projects, sooner or later you will have to fix two pieces of timber together. However, joints do not need to be overly complicated to be strong and accurate.

BUTT JOINTS

As long as the pieces of timber are perfectly clean and flat, these uncomplicated joints are the quickest way of joining two pieces of timber. To make a butt joint, hold two pieces of timber together, drill and countersink a pilot hole and add a dab of glue, then screw (or nail) the pieces together. If necessary, reinforce the joint with metal 'T' plates or corner braces.

Butt joints are strong enough to secure this rustic wooden bench without the need for corner braces.

MITRED JOINTS

In its simplest form, a mitre joint is just a butt joint at 45 degrees. It gives a neater finish on picture frames and architrave mouldings. To make a mitred joint, cut 45 degrees into both ends of the timber, hold these together and drill and countersink a pilot hole. Screw the two pieces of timber together.

FIXING BLOCKS

These are used to join boards or timbers at right angles to one another. They are very inexpensive and simple to fit and so they are probably the easiest way to make a strong and secure fixing. Fixing blocks are used to secure kitchen work surfaces and for rows of shelving.

SHELVING

This is the quickest and easiest way of increasing storage capacity in any home. As so many shelves end up being heavily overburdened, make sure you fix them firmly in the first place. Shelves were fitted into a narrow alcove in the Bloomsbury bedroom (see page 124) to provide additional storage.

▪ Determine the height of each shelf and cut the shelves to fit the width and depth of the alcove. To keep each shelf horizontal, use a spirit level and use the battens themselves and a pencil to mark out the positions for the battens to run around the three alcove walls.

Shelves were fitted into this alcove to provide extra storage space.

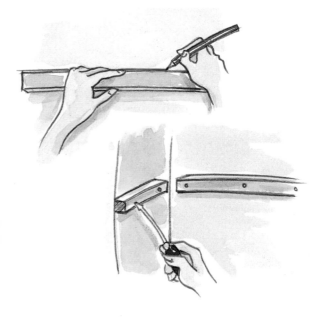

▪ Cut and drill timber battens and countersink the holes. Drill holes into the walls and use the correct rawlplugs (consult your hardware supplier) to fill the holes. Screw the battens to the wall. Rest the shelves on top of the battens (screw down from the top of the shelf into the batten, if necessary).

▪ Countersink holes, then screw a 5cm (2in) MDF strip (6mm/¼in), measured and cut to size with a jigsaw, to the front of each shelf. Prime the shelves and edging, then paint a cream emulsion base over the top. Once the base is dry, apply a top coat (we used the same terracotta colour wash as the walls).

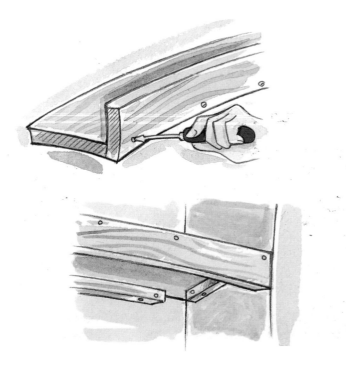

WINDOW FIXTURES & FITTINGS

Generally, on *Changing Rooms* we use an endless number of fixtures and fittings for window treatments. Here are some examples:

PELMET BOARDS & BOXES

For a deep pelmet board, fix a high shelf above the curtain track. Use metal 'L' shaped brackets for this, fitted at either end of the timber plank. Depending on the width of the pelmet, you may need to add another bracket in the centre.

To make a batten that holds a blind in position, cut a length of 5 x 2.5cm (2 x 1in) timber to the required width. Drill and countersink holes at either end of the timber and at the centre. For extra-long blinds, you may need additional holes. In the

Right: A fitted pelmet box conceals the top of this fabric blind. Pelmet boards (below) are used to swag luxurious lengths of fabric across window tops.

Mexican Kitchen (see pages 136–143), Andy secured the batten with four screws. Place the batten against the wall with a spirit level to check the horizontal. Mark the positions of the screws carefully with a pencil. Screw into the wall, then remove the pelmet and drill and rawlplug the holes. Finally, screw the pelmet into place.

A box pelmet is the same length as the curtain or blind batten and the returns are the depth of the curtain header plus 5cm (2in) for clearance. The three sides are secured with fixing blocks and a top is added to make a closed box that is lifted onto the batten and screwed into position to conceal unsightly fixings.

CURTAIN POLES

Plastic curtain poles are easy to install and are supplied with instructions. As curtains can be such an integral part of your room, why not make your own or choose a decorative pole? There are endless varieties of poles at most department stores. All poles are fixed with brackets to hold them in place and are usually supplied with rings and finials.

TILES & FLOORING

When tiling small areas like the Peckham dining room fireplace (see page 83) or a floor area, always measure the longest width of the area and the longest length to give you the maximum square meterage (yardage). Divide the square coverage of a single tile or a pack of tiles into this measurement to determine the number of tiles or packs required. Andy recommends that you use a profile gauge for cutting tiles to fit into awkward spaces.

Use the correct tiling adhesive and grout for the job. Wall and floor tiles need separate products, so always check the packaging before you buy. Spread bonding adhesive onto the surface with a notched spreader and press the tiles firmly into this. Use tile spacers to keep the interstices regularly balanced. When the adhesive is dry, spread grout over the surface of the tiles using a rubber-bladed squeegee. Remove the excess grout with a cloth and buff.

Hardboard flooring is suitable for smaller rooms (see page 88). Use flooring hardboard and staple or nail each piece tightly up to its neighbour. Work a power sander along the edges of each piece of hardboard to secure it in position. The hardboard is usually painted afterwards.

WORKING WITH ELECTRICITY

We always leave the electrics to the professional electricians and our ideas are carefully checked through. For the twiggy chandelier in Belsize Park (see page 32), an electrician split the central pendant light five ways with an electric connector block. These were secured on the top side of the twig out of sight. Five pendant bulbs were fitted to the connector blocks and dangled through the twiggy branch. We made sure that the dry twigs were not in contact with the naked bulbs.

You should only drill into a wall if you are confident that there are no cables running beneath the surface. If you are in any doubt, use a cable tester (available from DIY stores). This will illuminate when it is placed directly over a cable.

> Always follow the manufacturer's instructions when wiring new appliances. Unless the appliance is double-insulated (this will be stated on the packaging), do not forget to earth it. Replace broken plugs and frayed cables before they become hazardous. If you remove a plug from a socket and it still feels warm, there is likely to be a loose connection and the plug should therefore be rewired. When rewiring plugs, follow the manufacturer's diagram or check with your supplier.

ADVANCED CONSTRUCTION TECHNIQUES

When removing a staircase to install a loft ladder (see page 98), we got advice from the professionals. For a loft ladder, you will not always need planning permission but if you attempt any major work such as removing whole staircases or knocking down walls, we recommend that you seek the advice of a building surveyor and obtain the necessary permissions before work begins. Your local council will be able to supply you with further details of qualified building surveyors.

GENERAL GUIDE TO SAFETY

When carrying out any DIY, safety must be considered at all times. Every job that is carried out on *Changing Rooms* is checked and double-checked by professionals.

LADDERS

When using ladders, choose one that allows you to access the highest point that needs to be reached. Where a step ladder is not high enough, use a combination ladder that will convert into a step ladder. Never rest a ladder against glass. Use an 'S' shaped hook to hang a paint kettle or container from a ladder when you are working. You should also never lunge sideways whilst you are on a ladder or it will almost certainly topple over.

Occasionally, we have hired scaffolding towers in preference to using conventional ladders as in the Attic Room (pages 16–23) and Master Bedroom (pages 24–31). Both these rooms had tall ceilings and decking boards, fitted across scaffolds, made the work much safer and easier.

WORKING WITH ELECTRICITY

Whenever we change the lighting and use electrical equipment on the programme it is under the guidance of a qualified electrician. Always get an electrician to check any electrical equipment that has recently been installed.

Electrical equipment that is designed for DIY use should be correctly earthed. Never allow flex to run under carpets or staple it into position and never trail flex across floors. Always buy equipment that displays the kitemark (the British mark of safety). In the event of an emergency, switch off the electricity supply by operating the main switch on the consumer unit.

WORKING WITH ELECTRICAL APPLIANCES

When working with power tools, keep electric flexes out of the way. Always work in good light, take your time and never force a power tool. When using the following appliances, always wear safety goggles:

POWER SAWS

Always check that the blade is the right way round when fitting it. Do not remove the saw from the wood until it has stopped. Protect your work surface or use a work bench. Never use blunt, bent or damaged blades. When the saw blade is moving at full speed, begin cutting.

POWER DRILLS

Make a small hole with a nail punch or bradawl to provide a starting place for the drill. Use the drill at medium speed for small masonry holes or at slower speed for harder masonry. Exert a steady pressure and keep the drill at right angles to the wall. Remove the drill occasionally to clear debris and to cool the bit.

POWER SANDERS

Move the sander along the wood grain in overlapping strips. The machine moves the sanding paper in tiny circles, so finish sanding by hand, following the direction of the grain.

USING PAINTS & SOLVENTS

Wear safety goggles to protect your eyes from flying paint particles or rust, particularly when a surface is being prepared for painting. If you are using chemical paint or varnish stripper, protect your hands by wearing thick rubber gloves and if there is a lot of dust in the air (when sanding, for example) wear a safety mask too. Keep the room in which you are working well ventilated. Water-based products are less of a hazard but if you have sensitive skin you still need to wear protective gloves. When working with chemical strippers, keep pets and small children out of the way. If you get stripper on your skin, wash it off immediately with cold water.

VENTILATING ROOMS

Whatever type of paint you choose, always make sure that you ventilate the room in which you are working. Keep the windows fully open and, if possible, leave them open until the walls are thoroughly dry. Try to work outdoors if possible whenever you use chemical strippers, spray paints, glues or varnishes and always wear a protective face mask.

PAINT LISTINGS

Below is an alphabetical room-by-room listing of the paints used in the featured rooms:

ARTS & CRAFTS DINING ROOM

WALLS: Homebase vinyl matt emulsion (Chantilly) and Homebase matt emulsion (Fern Green).
STENCIL: Dulux vinyl matt emulsion matchpots: 3070 Y70R, 4050 Y50R/3070 and Y80R/2040 Y020R.

ATTIC MUSIC ROOM

WALLS: Dulux 'Once' vinyl matt emulsion (Magnolia), Sanderson vinyl matt emulsion (Tawny Desert) 5-11M and Sanderson vinyl matt emulsion (Ming Gold) 5-5M.
SUN: Sanderson vinyl matt emulsion (Andean Grey) 44-24D.
CEILING: Sanderson vinyl matt emulsion (Blue Day) 24-15M.

BLOOMSBURY BEDROOM

WALLS: Base coat is Crown Expressions matt emulsion (Snowflake) and top coat is watered-down ochre, olive, mauve and terracotta mixed from Sandersons matchpots: Empire Gold 6-12D, Congo Red 15-24D, Livery 20-12D, Blue Velvet 24-24D, Mandarin Blue 25-6D, Etruscan Red 16-24D, Basque Brown 6-24D, Golden Meadow 41-14D and Dewberry 56-18U.
FURNITURE: Base is Snowflake and details are Sanderson as above.

COUNTRY BEDROOM

WALLS: Dulux 'Once' emulsion (Brilliant White) and Stencil Store colour wash (Stonewash White) from Homebase.
FLOOR: Homebase quick-drying satinwood (Mink) and thinned emulsion (White) with added scumble glaze.
WARDROBES: Crown Expressions vinyl matt emulsion (Regal Blue) U3-50.

FENG SHUI BEDROOM

WALLS: Dulux vinyl matt emulsion 5040 G50Y.
Colour used behind copper leaf: Sanderson vinyl matt emulsion (Royal Blue) 27-6D.

GOTHIC BEDROOM

WALLS: Sanderson vinyl matt emulsion (Gobi Tan) 6-23M, Sanderson vinyl matt emulsion (Basque Brown) 6-24D and Sanderson vinyl matt emulsion (Algerian Red) 54-5U.
FLOOR CLOTH: Sanderson vinyl matt emulsion (Princess Blue) 54-21U.

LOFT BEDROOM

WALLS: Sanderson matt emulsion 41-6D (Mayan Green).
WALL DECORATION: Sanderson spectrum matt emulsion (Spinach Green).
WOODWORK: Sanderson W4-3M vinyl silk (Cloudy Amber).

MASTER BEDROOM

WALLS: Dulux (Cornfield) 764Y13 R.
CEILING COLOURS: Dulux oil-based

undercoat (White), Do It All satin sheen (Atlantic Blue), Do It All satin sheen (Magnolia).
DOORS AND WOODWORK: Black gloss.
SHUTTERS: Crown Solo satin (Wild Beige).

MEXICAN KITCHEN

WALLS: Base is vinyl silk (Magnolia) and top coat is Crown Expressions (Flambeau) F320 plus scumble glaze.
CUPBOARDS: Crown Expressions matt emulsion (Blue Pencil) and Colron liquid wax (Dark Oak).

MULTI-PURPOSE BEDROOM

WALLS: Base coat is Dulux vinyl matt emulsion (Lady Mantle) 1040 G70Y; top coat is Dulux vinyl matt emulsion 1020 G70Y (Chinois) and 1060 G70Y (Sundew).
BUNK BEDS: Dulux vinyl matt emulsion (Achievement) 2060 R80B.
CHEST: Chinois (as walls).

MULTI-PURPOSE GUEST ROOM

WALLS: Sanderson vinyl matt emulsion (Lemon Whip) 6-1P.
DOORS AND SKIRTINGS: Sanderson vinyl matt emulsion (New Green) 40-1P.
CUPBOARD DOORS: Sanderson vinyl matt emulsion (Spicy Green) 40-6D and Sanderson vinyl matt emulsion (Brilliant Tangerine).

NAUTICAL ATTIC ROOM

WALLS AND DOORS: Dulux vinyl matt emulsion (Brilliant White)

and Dulux vinyl matt emulsion 0030 G10Y (Folklore) 0030 G10Y.
WOODWORK: Dulux vinyl matt emulsion (Brilliant White), Polyvine Classic colour effects from B & Q and acrylic artist's colours from art stores.
SHELVES: Cuprinol wood stain (Green).

PERIOD-LOOK DINING ROOM

WALLS: Fads Homestyle vinyl matt emulsion (Barley White).
WOODWORK: Base coat is Fads Homestyle non-drip gloss (Jade); top coat is Fads Homestyle on-coat gloss (Pacific Blue).

RESTFUL LIVING ROOM

WALLS: Crown matt emulsion (Ivanhoe) B1-70, Crown matt emulsion (Kohlrabi) B1-80, Cameo Pink and Ginger Whip matchpots.

TURQUOISE BEDROOM

WALLS: Dulux Definitions Heritage range matt emulsion 1050 B50G (M'Ladies Room).
FIREPLACE: Quick-dry matt black emulsion and Silver treasure wax from Tiranti's of Warren Street.
FLOOR: watered-down matt emulsion (White).

VICTORIAN FORMAL ROOM

WALLS: Dulux Heritage matt emulsion (Crimson Red), matt emulsion (Black) and scumble glaze.
CEILING: Dulux 'Once' matt emulsion (Brilliant White).

STOCKISTS & SUPPLIERS

The following companies and organizations have supplied materials and equipment to *Changing Rooms*.

ARCHITECTURAL ANTIQUES LTD., Victoria Mills, Stainland Road, Greetland, Halifax, West Yorks. HX4 8AD. (01422) 377314.

ARTHUR SANDERSON & SONS LTD., 112/120 Brompton Road, Knightsbridge, London SW3 1JJ. (0171) 584 3344. (For paints and fabrics.)

B & Q, 1 Hampshire Corporate Park, Chandlers Ford, Eastleigh, Hants. SO53 3YX. (01703) 256256.

BARNETT & LAWSON TRIMMINGS, 16/17 Little Portland Street, London W1N 6NE. (0171) 636 8591. (Mail order service.)

BHS, Marylebone House, 129/137 Marylebone Road, London NW1 5QD. (0171) 262 3288.

BMJ POWER LTD. (0345) 230230. (For power tools.)

BOROVICKS, 16 Berwick Street, London W1V 4HP. (0171) 437 2180. (For fabrics.)

BRATS, 281 Kings Road, London SW3 5EW. (For paints.)

CROWN PAINTS, P.O. Box 37, Crown House, Hollins Road, Darwen, Lancs. BB3 2BG. (01254) 704951.

DO IT ALL (Freephone 0500 300321.

DULUX PAINTS, The Dulux Advice Centre, ICI Paints, Woxham Road, Slough, Berks. SL2 5DS. (01753) 550555.

DYLON INTERNATIONAL LTD. (Consumer Advice Line: 0181 663 4296.)

FARROW & BALL, Uddens Trading Estate, Wimborne, Dorset BH21 7NL.

GEORGE WEIL & SONS LTD., The Warehouse, 20 Reading Arch Road, Redhill, Surrey RH1 1HG. (01737) 778868.

HABITAT STORE INFORMATION LINE: (0645) 334433 (calls charged at local rate).

HOMEBASE LTD., Stamford House, Stamford Street, London SE1 9LL. (0171) 921 6000.

HSS HIRE SHOPS (0800) 282 8282. (For floor sanders and other hire equipment, phone this number for your local branch.)

IKEA, 2 Drury Way, North Circular Road, London NW10 0TH. (0181 208 5600). (Ring for branches.)

JALI, Apsley House, Chartham, Canterbury, Kent. (01277) 831710. (Mail order service.)

JOHN LEWIS PARTNERSHIP, 278/306 Oxford Street, London W1A 1EX. (0171) 629 7711.

LAKELAND PLASTICS, Alexandra Buildings, Windermere, Cumbria LA23 1BQ. (015394) 88100. (Mail order service.)

LASSCO., St Michael's Church, Mark Street, London EC2A 4ER. (0171) 739 0448. (For salvage yards.)

LIBERON, Mountfield Industrial Estate, New Romney, Kent TN28 8XU. (Technical hotline: (01797) 367555 open weekdays 9.30 am–4.30 pm) (For waxes and stains.)

MALABAR, 31/33 The South Bank Business Centre, Ponton Road, London SW8 5BL. (0171) 501 4210. (Fabric suppliers.)

MOSAIC WORKSHOP, 443 Holloway Road, London N7 3LJ. (0171) 263 2997. (Mail order service.)

THE NATURAL FABRIC COMPANY, Wessex Place, 127 High Street, Hungerford RG17 00L. (01488) 684002.
(For fabrics by mail order.)

NICE IRMA'S, Finchley Industrial Centre, High Road, London N12 8QA. (0181) 343 9590. (Mail order service.)

PAPERCHASE, 213 Tottenham Court Road, London W1P 9AF. (0171) 580 8496.

PAPERS AND PAINTS, 4 Park Walk, London SW10 0AD. (0171) 352 8606.

THE PIER, 91/95 Kings Road, London SW3 4PA. (0171) 351 7100. (Ring for branches.)

PLASTERWORKS, 38 Cross Street, London N1 2BG. (0171) 226 5355.

PLASTI-KOTE LTD., London Road Industrial Estate, Saston, Cambridge CB2 4TR. (01223) 836400. (For spray paints, enamels, etc.)

POLYVINE, Vine House, Rockhampton, Berkeley, Glos. GL13 9DT. (01454) 261276.

RJ'S HOMESHOPS, 209 Tottenham Court Road, London W1P 9AF. (0171) 637 7474.

RONSEAL LTD., Thorncliffe Road, Chapeltown, Sheffield S30 4YP. (0114) 2467171. (For varnishes.)

RUSSELL & CHAPPLE, 23 Monmouth Street, London WC1. (0171) 836 7521. (Mail order service.)

RYMANS, Ryman House, Swallowfield Way, Hayes, Middlesex UB3 1DQ. (0181) 569 3000. (For mail order, call (0800) 801901.)

SALVO, Ford Woodhouse, Berwick on Tweed, Northumberland TD15 2QF (01668) 216494. (Architectural listings magazine.)

SELFRIDGES, 400 Oxford Street, London W1A 1AA. (0171) 629 1234.

THE STENCIL STORE GROUP PLC., 20/21 Heronsgate Road, Chorleywood, Herts. WD3 5BN. (01923) 28557788.

ALEC TIRANTI LTD., 70 High Street, Theale, Reading RG7 5AR. (0118) 930 2775 or 27 Warren Street, London W1P 5DG. (0171) 636 8565. (Shops and mail order.)

WALCOT RECLAMATION, The Depot, Riverside Business Park, Lower Bristol Road, Bath BA2 3DW. (01225) 335532. (SAE for brochure.)

WICKES BUILDING SUPPLIES LTD., Station Road, Harrow, Middlesex HA1 2QB. (Freefone (0500) 300328.)

WOLFIN TEXTILES, 64 Great Titchfield Street, London W1P 7AE. (0171) 636 4949.

GLOSSARY

The following is a list of useful DIY terms used in the book and throughout the decorating industry.

BATTEN: A timber strip used to secure timber, MDF or fabric securely onto a wall surface.

BEADING: a narrow (usually wooden) decorative edging strip.

BEVEL: a slanting edge, such as the shape of a chisel.

BUTT JOINT: where two edges touch without overlapping.

CALICO: a thin, unbleached cotton.

CHALKLINE: a piece of string coated with chalk which is snapped onto a surface to leave a precise line.

CORNICE: a decorative moulding covering the join between the ceiling and the wall.

COUNTERSINK: to widen the outer edge of a drilled hole into a cone shape to allow a screwhead to be sunk below the surface.

DADO RAIL: a rail fixed to the lower half of the wall above the skirting board.

DECOUPAGE: coloured or black and white cut-out images, cut from their background paper and pasted onto a surface for decoration and then sealed with varnish.

DOWNLIGHTERS: recessed spotlights in the ceiling that cast light in a downwards direction.

FINIAL: an decorative attachment placed at each end of a curtain pole to prevent the rings from falling off.

FRETWORK: intricate, decoratively-shaped wood or MDF.

GILDING: the art of applying gold paint or gold leaf to furniture or a wooden frame.

GOLD SIZE: an adhesive layer that is used to bond gold or metal leaf onto a surface.

GROUTING: a thin mortar used to seal the joins between tiles.

KEY: to roughen a surface to improve adhesion before painting.

LAMINATE: layers of different substances pressed together and strengthened to make a tough surface material.

MATT: a flat paint finish.

MDF: medium-density fibreboard, available in sheet form for cutting or as pre-cut mouldings and grilles.

MELAMINE: a sprayed-on plastic coating usually applied to chip-board for a low-cost material.

MITRE: to trim the ends of wood, plaster or fabric to form a 45-degree angle so that when two ends are joined together they form a perfect right angle.

MOIRE: a patterned surface rather like rippled silk.

MOULDING: a length of wood shaped to form a decorative strip.

PELMET: shaped and stiffened drapery fitted across the top of a window. It is used ornamentally to hide curtain rails.

PELMET BOARD: a horizontal board used to support the pelmet and sometimes used as a base to support swags and tails.

PIPING CORD: soft cotton cord used to finish a seamed edge.

PLUMB LINE: a string for testing the perpendicularity of a line.

POLYURETHANE: a plastic resin made to strengthen varnishes.

RETURN: the part of a curtain or pelmet that turns around the sides.

ROUNDEL: a round shape that is constructed or drawn onto a wall or ceiling.

SANDING: smoothing with rough sandpaper.

SCUMBLING: a broken paintwork effect for walls and furniture.

SPIRIT LEVEL: a glass tube which is partly filled with spirit. It is used to test whether a surface is horizontal.

SWAG: a generous scoop of fabric that hangs from two fixed points over a window or bed.

TEMPLATE: a pattern cut to a specific dimension and used as an outline for cutting the same shape from another material.

TIE BACK: a shapened and stiffened band, tasselled cord or ribbon used to hold back curtains.

TONGUE-AND-GROOVE: wooden boards with a groove along one edge and a protruding tongue down the other. The tongue slots into the groove of an adjacent piece for a secure fixing.

WADDING: a soft, bulky material used for stuffing shapes.

WALL PLUG OR RAWLPLUG: an expandable plastic encasement for a screw. A plug is inserted into a pre-drilled hole to provide a gripping surface for the screw.

INDEX

AUTHOR'S ACKNOWLEDGEMENTS

I would like to thank all the designers whose work is represented in this book for the skill and enthusiasm that has gone into each of their rooms. Thank you to Jane Donovan for the time and patience which has gone into getting this book to press and to Jane Forster for her talented design work. Thanks also to Shona Wood for her photography and to Adam Woods, Jake Robinson, Sally Barker, Gabriel Mossa, Mark Thurgood, Marco Crevello and Crispin Snowdon.

I would particularly like to thank Ann Hill and Pauline Doidge, the Producers of *Changing Rooms*, Linda Clifford, the Executive Producer and Assistant Producers Susannah Walker and Andrew Anderson for their talent in making a successful programme, on which it has been a pleasure to work. And thanks to Baz for getting it right in the first place.

The book production team would like to thank the following people: Barnhouse Veterinary Surgery, Chester (for supplying branches of blossom), Sarah Coles and Martin Leach, Anne at the Early Learning Centre, Sovereign Centre, Weston Super Mare (for supplying props), Anne Hay, Dino at IDM Computers, Gerald at Neal Street East, Neal Street, Covent Garden, London WC2 (for supplying props), F.A. Pollak Ltd., Unit 3, Rosebery House, 70 Rosebery Avenue, London EC1R 4RR (for gold frame samples), Stragglethorpe Hall (for splendid accommodation) and the Welsh College of Horticulture, Northop, Mold, Clwyd, Wales (for supplying flowers). We would also like to thank all the neighbours who were so hospitable and understanding.